For Sharon

- a good critic and a good friend.

Paul

# THE HAPPY CRITIC
## and Other Essays

*By the same author*

POETRY

Collected Poems—Jonathan Gentry—A Winter Diary—Mortal Summer—The Mayfield Deer—The Seven Sleepers and Other Poems—New Poems—Spring Birth and Other Poems—Morning Worship and Other Poems—Selected Poems

FICTION

The Short Stories of Mark Van Doren—The Witch of Ramoth and Other Tales—Nobody Say a Word and Other Stories—Home with Hazel and Other Stories—The Transients—Windless Cabins—Tilda

NONFICTION

Henry David Thoreau—John Dryden—The Private Reader—Shakespeare—Liberal Education—The Noble Voice—Nathaniel Hawthorne—Introduction to Poetry—An Anthology of World Poetry—Don Quixote's Profession—The Autobiography of Mark Van Doren

DRAMA

The Last Days of Lincoln

# THE HAPPY CRITIC
## and Other Essays

*by* MARK VAN DOREN

HILL AND WANG · NEW YORK

Library of Congress catalog card number 61-14476

FIRST EDITION

Manufactured in the United States of America

To
Robert Caldwell

# Preface

THE short piece with which this book begins, and from which it takes its title, will not I hope mislead anyone into supposing that I consider myself a professional critic or that I practice the art with indiscriminate, incessant pleasure. Nearly twenty years ago, in the preface to a collection of essays and reviews called *The Private Reader*, I said good-by to criticism and explained why I did so: I was done with the desire, and no longer felt at home in the field. Henceforth, I announced, I would read for myself as most people do and refrain from making my opinions public.

But here are these further essays to prove the announcement premature. In a sense I continue to think that it was not; most of the time I still am a private reader, and find it charming to be one. Yet how can I deny that upon a number of occasions I have come back to the desk, or it may be to the lectern, and carried on about things pertaining to literature? With this difference, though: the emphasis now is upon the root rather than the branch, the general rather than the particular truth, if truth at all. I have to be sure discussed particular men: Whitman, Hardy, Mann, Cervantes, and Herrick. The reason in each case, however, was as much what the writer represented as what he wrote. And if in the course of the book I say certain things more than once, more even than twice, I am content to let the repetition stand, since it underlines my beliefs and leaves less doubt as to what they are.

Not to sound too sober at this moment, I make haste to agree once more with Mr. Eliot that for the normal critic, or as I would say the happy critic, the purpose of literature is to amuse. If that word feels too light, then substitute another: entertain. And if this word still feels light, then remember that it is only the mind which in human beings is ever entertained. Entertainment is a tremendous as well as a delightful thing, and there are plenty of writers, God knows, who do not succeed at it. My present search could be called, I suppose, a search for the principles of entertainment: a serious subject but not in my view a solemn one, nor one susceptible, say, to scientific treatment.

I have begun with four short pieces, not simply one, in the faith that they state for me the themes of the longer work to come. They do this incompletely, and of course I must not exaggerate the unity of a collection whose parts have depended for their existence upon more or less random occasions. Yet in the main I find that my deepest convictions are somehow expressed here. "The Possible Importance of Poetry" and the lecture on *Leaves of Grass* will appear, I trust, to complement rather than contradict each other; between them they deal with the distinction, so vital yet so difficult to draw, between subject matter and art. The lecture on Hardy's poems considers a tragic artist, and those on Mann and Cervantes do all they can to show how the comic genius functions. "The Artist and the Changing World" asks artists to be responsible in their claims for special treatment by society. "The Kinds of Knowledge" will suggest that there is common ground on which the scholar and the layman both may stand. Then the two final pieces, diversions if you please, take off from visits I made with my wife to Greece and England in 1955.

The two terms that recur most often in these pages are tragedy and comedy. They are a pair, of course: the most famous pair in either literature or life. Together they yield the largest subject that anyone I think could discuss, for the division between them goes down to the very bottom of things, at least as men see things and report them. I might have added a long essay on this subject; but it would have been longer than the book. For twelve years I lectured on tragedy and comedy at Columbia University, and I never thought I had exhausted the subject, let alone fairly begun it. Nor is it a subject that can be treated systematically, with definitions available at the finish. Tragedy and comedy can no more be defined than life and death can, or love and truth. For one thing, they are different and yet the same. They are twin ways of dealing with human error: the only concern of story when it is serious. One works with darkness and the other with light, one with deeds and the other with the contemplation of deeds; but those opposites are close together, and sometimes they change places. *Hamlet* is light with brilliance and wit; *Don Quixote* is unaccountably sad. The essay I should have written I never will. I bequeath it to a bolder spirit, comforting myself meanwhile with the assurance that I have delivered glancing blows at the subject on many pages of this book, as well as in *Shakespeare*, where it was naturally a central consideration, then later in *The Noble Voice*, especially in the chapters on Homer and Chaucer, and still later in *Nathaniel Hawthorne*. It might be that glancing blows are the only kind which can hope to count. Yet the direct attack may be possible too. Whoever undertakes it has my admiring and envious good wishes.

MARK VAN DOREN

Cornwall Hollow
Connecticut
1961

# Acknowledgments

THE first three items in this collection are reprinted from *The Nation*, 1949–1950, and the fourth from the *Sewanee Review*, Winter 1945. "The Possible Importance of Poetry" was read as the Hopwood Lecture, 1951, at the University of Michigan; it was printed in the *Michigan Alumnus Quarterly Review*, Summer 1951, and reprinted in *The Writer and His Craft*, The University of Michigan Press, 1954. "Leaves of Grass: 1855–1955" was read at the Library of Congress on January 17, 1955, under the auspices of the Gertrude Clarke Whittall Poetry and Literature Fund; it was printed by the Library in a pamphlet, *Walt Whitman: Man, Poet, Philosopher*, 1955, and bore the title there "The Poet." "The Poems of Thomas Hardy" was read at the Johns Hopkins Poetry Festival, November 1958, and printed in *Four Poets on Poetry*, The Johns Hopkins Press, 1959. "Joseph and His Brothers" was read at Bryn Mawr College, October 1956; was published by Caroline Newton in a pamphlet, *The Thomas Mann Commemoration*, Philadelphia, 1956; and was reprinted in the *American Scholar*, Summer 1957. "Don Quixote's Profession" was read as three lectures at Emory University in November 1956 and was published as a book by the Columbia University Press, 1958. "The Artist and the Changing World," read as the Blashfield Address at the American Academy of Arts and Letters in May 1951, was printed in the *Proceedings* of the Academy, 1952, and reprinted in *Seven Arts*, 1953. "The Kinds of Knowledge" was read at the first Bicentennial Convocation of Columbia University, January

1954, and printed in the *American Scholar*, Autumn 1955. The last two items appeared in *The Reporter* under different titles from those used here: "The Glory That Is Still Greece," January 12, 1956, and "A Visit to the Home of Robert Herrick," March 22, 1956. Acknowledgment of all these sources is hereby gratefully made.

# Contents

# The Happy Critic

A GOOD critic, like a good poet, is made as well as born. It is impossible to imagine him without education and experience, or even erudition. He has learned how to do what he does. But he was born, too—born able to learn, and to delight in the exercise of his art. He also is an artist, and as such will never be competent wholly to explain his processes, or to teach others how they may imitate them. It is as hard, or almost as hard, to know how a fine critic arrived at his result as it is to know how a great poem or story took shape in its author's mind. The rest of us had read the work the critic read, just as all of us have lived the life the poet lived; yet we had failed to notice certain things, or to see how they combined with other things to produce the final effect which now, in the critic's words, is clearly before us.

A good critic, then, is born as well as made; and Ben Jonson, whom I paraphrase, would not I think protest the conversion of his terms. I am not so sure about my own contemporaries. Their perpetual discussion of what criticism is rarely pauses for contemplation of the fact, if it is a fact, that good critics are rare and wonderful, and not easily explained. To me it is a fact, and I take pleasure in contemplating it. The method of a given critic, or his knowledge, or his seriousness—these are important things to consider, but the sum of them is a little less important than the presence in him of genius if he has it. If he hasn't it, nothing else that he has will save him in the long run.

Genius in a critic is sense. I do not mean common sense, though that is a great thing; nor do I mean anything negative. Of course the good critic is no kind of fool, and of course he has what all men have in common; but these are not enough. I suppose I mean wisdom—the fullest, the most natural, the freest and happiest sense of what is true. The good critic is free of his knowledge and his method. And he is free of the delusion that he can explain everything in the author he treats, or that he can say once and for all what literature is, has been, should be. His seriousness does not make him dull; rather, it makes him light—not heavy, at any rate. He may not know what literature is, but he does know how it lives and breathes, and how it can make us happy. He himself knows how to be happy in the way that none but serious persons are. Not cheerful, not complacent, not easily pleased; but *when* pleased, capable of joy. We cannot take seriously one who is incapable of joy.

The foregoing must sound strange in this grim time when literature is so seldom enjoyed. By the critics, anyway. It is all work for them and no play, and I have actually encountered laymen—neither writers nor critics—who thought them dull boys. Let us not say that, but let us regret with T. S. Eliot that it has become so difficult in recent decades for anyone to be what he calls a "normal critic." Dryden for Mr. Eliot was such a critic. He practiced the art "before writing about poetry had come to mean philosophizing about it, . . . at a time when neither the fundamental nature of the poetic activity nor the social function of poetry was yet considered the subject matter of literary criticism. . . . In that happy age it did not occur to him to inquire what poetry was *for*, how it affected the nerves of listeners, how it sublimated the wishes of the poet, whom it should satisfy, and all the other questions which really have nothing to do with poetry as poetry; and the poet was not expected to be either a sibyl or a prophet. The purpose of poetry and drama was to *amuse;* but it was to amuse properly; and the larger forms of poetry should have a moral significance; by exhibiting the thoughts and passions of man through lively image and melodious verse, to edify and to refine the reader and auditor."

"I do not know," adds Mr. Eliot, "that we have improved upon this conception of the place and function of poetry." Indeed we have not, but it is depressing to note how few of Mr. Eliot's admirers have been moved by what he says here, and to realize how many of them must have jumped to his implied conclusion that it was easy in Dryden's time to do what Dryden did. No one else was doing it. Thomas Rymer, for instance, was doing the dull things we do, with enormous industry and impressive system; he was applying "the rules" to Shakespeare. He was not without merit, either; but he lacked the genius which in Dryden showed as ease, good nature, wit, and the simple power to see greatness wherever greatness was. Dryden must have seemed to Rymer a careless amateur, without true consistency or a statable plan. Yet he was the first to praise Shakespeare and Chaucer as we praise them now. Judging by the critical equipment he exposed, he should not have known how to do this. But he did know, and that is everything.

Also, he was a master of prose. A good critic must be a good writer, and it is no accident that this is so. I suspect that Rymer was sometimes infuriated by the success of Dryden's essays. It was among other things a literary success; people were ravished by their grace, as people still are. But again this was no accident. Art cannot be praised except by those who have the language; who can say things worthy of their subjects; who can be compendious and memorable; who themselves, though in another mode, are artists too. Rymer, who thought the business of the critic was to instruct the poet against negligence and miscarriage, expressed the fear in 1674 that "some critics are like wasps, that rather annoy the bees than terrify the drones." It did not occur to him that critics can be drones. They can be, even now.

# The Happy Poet

THE HAPPY poet is like the courageous man whom Socrates defined: he knows what to fear and what not to fear from the critic who will tell him what he should have written. Or written about, for the subject is the thing; and in our time the subject *is* the time. The poet is supposed to have a relation to his time beyond the relation which consists of having been born in it like all other living men. A conscious, cultivated relation which it is the chief business of his poems to express—that is what the critic looks for, and so seldom likes. For he also is having his relation, his love affair, with the age; and if last year he thought it was one thing that made the contemporary world go round, this year he has changed his mind; it is another thing, and the poet seems not to have heard of it yet. So the poet is asked, not too politely, to take a seat in the learner's row; or he is told right out that he will never do at all and might as well die now. As an artist he is already six months dead, and that in the modern calendar is as near eternity as man will get.

The happy poet is the one who knows how much of this is nonsense. Not all of it is. The poet, as a poet, who is not alive now will never be alive. But what is being alive, and how much can we afford to worry about it? The happy poet does not worry any more. For one thing he has stopped reading criticism; and for another he has bravely decided what is nonsense and what is not nonsense with respect to the duty of being up to date. It has ceased in fact to be a duty; he has learned to like being alive, not only in his own time but in time itself, of which he now is master as only poets can be masters of man's worst enemy and best friend. He is able to understand St. Augustine's remark: all times are similar insofar as they are times. And paraphrasing Mr. Eliot, he can say the good poet is one who knows when to be conscious and when to be unconscious of the world he is told he lives in.

He must be conscious of it when he has to consider its uniqueness, but he had better be unconscious of it when it resembles other worlds, as most of the time it does. Every age is an individual, yet no age can be a pure individual; if one were, there would be nothing to say about it, even for critics. The critics who discuss our age betray by doing so their belief that it bears some resemblance to its older brothers, not to speak of brothers still unborn. They use language, and language cannot cope with the unique. The poet's language seems to—we say he makes individuals, and teaches them to talk—but *seems* is the word. Hamlet is himself; he is also a man; he is a man of his time; and he is a man of our time. The poet who made him was a happy poet, free both in and of his world. The historians who call him Elizabethan cannot explain why he is more intelligible than the other Elizabethans whom he resembled.

Of course he resembled them; but if he had been identical with them their age would not be now as famous as it is. It is famous because it produced this poet who above all other poets comprehended what it means to live in time as well as in a time. It means, for instance, that one remembers—or by coincidence recalls—things thought and uttered long ago. "My lord, I will use them according to their desert." "God's bodykins, man, better. Use every man after his desert, and who should escape whipping? Use them after your own honor and dignity. The less they deserve, the more merit is in your bounty." That is Elizabethan, but better yet, it is true. It was true when Socrates and Christ said it, and it is true now when a few statesmen understand it. Only a few, but it only takes a few.

The criticism that scares readers away from poetry is the sort of criticism that would call this commonplace. And besides, it is in a play, and the play is about people. Poets today are not supposed to know about people, and to prove that they do by writing stories. Poets now are lyric poets—if even lyric, for music in words is suspect. The happy poet, lyric if he likes, is also free to be epic and dramatic; and free not to write as if the people of his time were like no other people who ever lived—lost generations, and such. Free, too, of the necessity to show by what he writes that he has had the approved experiences, of love and of hate, with the spirit of our age. What is the spirit of our age, and how nervous should the poet be lest he leave some echo of it out of even his best lines? Not nervous at all, the happy poet says. The best lines are best for absurdly ancient reasons; they are musical, and they are true. If this is trite, time too is trite. It never gets tired of changing and not changing, of resembling and differing from itself. Or of deciding—the old impostor—what is true.

# The Uses of Translation

ONE PIECE of pedantry we have with us always—a book is not read well unless it is read in its native tongue. Some go farther and say that only then is it read at all: Homer in English has nothing left of his greatness. And so with Dante. And so, presumably, with Cervantes, Rabelais, Montaigne, Pascal, Voltaire, Rousseau, Stendhal, Balzac, and Proust; so with Tolstoy and Dostoevsky; so with Ibsen; so with Goethe; so with Plutarch; so with Lucretius; so with Plato and Aristotle; so with Herodotus and Thucydides; so with St. Augustine and St. Thomas; so with Machiavelli and Molière. So too, of course, with the Bible. If you cannot read Hebrew you will never know anything about Abraham, and if you are not a master of first-century Greek you will have no notion of what Jesus said.

The list, which could be longer, itself reveals the pedantry. Many a person, speaking thus, forgets in his pride of knowing Greek that he knows no Hebrew; or, if he knows some Russian, that he did as a matter of fact first feel Raskolnikov's force through the English of Constance Garnett; or, granting that he reads Russian as Russians do, that he did once, in a moment of inadvertence, enjoy Li Po by way of Ezra Pound. But this is not the biggest mistake he makes. His true crime—the word is scarcely too strong—consists in his ignorance of how the literature of the world has exerted its power. It has exerted it—in the world—by being translated. Only great writers, to be sure, can be translated without deadly loss; the others, having at best a minor, a local virtue, die promptly in foreign air. But it is the great writers that count in the great world; for the great world understands, as none other does, the language of literature. There is the English language, but a few who have used it wrote also in the human tongue, and that tongue—witness Shakespeare—can be comprehended anywhere. Even we who are most vain of our knowledge that Shakespeare wrote English as no one else ever has can also take pleasure in contemplating that the Germans once did, and the Russians now do, consider him their best poet. To insist that he is only ours would be to deny his ultimate distinction. It would be, in fact, to expose our incapacity to see what that distinction is. It would prove that we read him badly even in English, as many classical scholars read Homer badly in Greek. They read him, that is to say, without suspecting his immense, his humorous, his natural, his wise, his temperate, his courageous power.

A recent translation of *Don Quixote* has been recommended as the first such translation to render in English the true meaning of that tremendous masterpiece. Those who say this, and by a certain logic they should add that *Don Quixote* should not have been translated at all, tell us that only now can we know—well, what the whole world has known about Cervantes for three hundred years. Comedy at its deepest and best is not a Spanish thing, it is a human thing, it is an intellectual and emotional thing, and somehow neither Fielding nor Dickens nor the author of *Huckleberry Finn* missed it; not to speak of a million other readers in whose minds the influence of Cervantes will never be traced. The influence of great literature is universal, and in the course of things works through translation. The Romans did not understand all the Greek they turned into Latin, but without the part they did understand they would have had no literature at all. The Elizabethan Age was ushered in by translations of Plutarch, Montaigne, Seneca, Ovid, and many another ancient or foreign writer without access to whom Shakespeare, for instance, would have been poorer. I have never heard it seriously suggested that he should not have tried his hand at *Julius Caesar* and *Antony and Cleopatra* because North's Plutarch was the only Plutarch he could read. Dryden's Virgil and Pope's Homer created an age of English poetry, just as French translations of English books caused 1789, and just as English translations of German books caused Transcendentalism.

I am told that I cannot know what Aristotle is saying in his *Poetics* unless my Greek is perfect, but I must refuse to believe this. I must admit, to be sure, the difficulty of rendering each term precisely as that greatest of literary critics intended it. But another sort of precision in him nobody can miss. It is the precision that guards his mind against the blunder of leaving any important consideration out as he decides what poetry—we would say story—at its fullest is. A complete story, he certainly is saying, will be good in its language, its characters, its scene, its sentiments, its ideas, and its plot—most of all its plot, which is its very soul, and indeed is always the thing an unwise poet manages worst. Modern criticism can praise a novelist or a playwright for one of these virtues alone, and regularly does. To do so is not to ask him for enough, and in the long run is not to get enough. Literature dries up without a living memory of what it is that happens when it uses all its power. Here, finally, is the one use of translation that outmeasures the others. It keeps us open to greatness wherever it may be, and it may be anywhere. As one literature withers another revives it; as one nation of writers forgets its chief business another nation shows it has remembered. Translation keeps literature going in the world. It always has, and it always will unless the pedants have their way. Of course they will not have their way.

# Poets and Trimmers

ONE of the hundred cantos in which *The Divine Comedy* describes a world is devoted with compendious scorn to those lost people who lived without blame and without praise, but were for themselves; who now have no hope of death; report of whom the world permits not to exist; who never had any "good of the intellect"; who from cowardice made the great refusal. Only one canto deals with these trimmers, and not even all of that; but Dante makes it clear how many of them there are—they are the majority of mankind—and how absolutely both he and Virgil despise them. "Regard, and pass." "I should never have believed death had undone so many."

We meet them in the third canto of the hundred, and we are not reminded of them again. The rest of the journey is among those who sinned or who did not sin; who chose between the only two alternatives faced by men, and according to their choice are now being punished or blessed. The trimmers are not even in Hell, as certainly they are not in Purgatory or Heaven. Dante has glanced at them and passed; he has other latitudes to climb, low, middle, and high. The vast world he will traverse dwarfs the very memory of that multitude which never lived, and which includes almost everybody. *The Divine Comedy* is about the relatively few who will live forever, either as sinners or as saints. Hell has its immortality, no less than the scented country beyond the river, in sight of the breathing Rose. There is ample escape from these suffocating regions of death and yet no death.

For the modern poet there is no such escape. He strangulates in a universe populated entirely by trimmers, and therefore, and everywhere, dead. There is no entrance into the earth which can conduct him to where some souls are interestingly damned; there is no mount beyond where in the sweet light he can see others happily punished; and still beyond this mount there is no ladder of arcs which he can ascend and be free of human place or time. He himself is condemned to live his whole life and do his whole work in the midst of a multitude he cannot but loathe.

"Let others complain that the age is wicked," wrote Kierkegaard in 1843; "my complaint is that it is wretched; for it lacks passion. Men's thoughts are thin and flimsy like lace, they are themselves pitiable like the lacemakers. The thoughts of their hearts are too paltry to be sinful. For a worm it might be regarded as a sin to harbor such thoughts, but not for a being made in the image of God. Their lusts are dull and sluggish, their passions sleepy. . . . This is the reason my soul always turns back to the Old Testament and to Shakespeare. I feel that those who speak there are at least human beings: they hate, they love, they murder their enemies, and curse their descendants throughout all generations, they sin."

"The modern world debases," wrote Charles Péguy a generation ago. "Other worlds had other occupations. Other worlds had other ulterior motives and other ulterior intentions. Other worlds had other temporal pastimes, between meals. The modern world debases. Other worlds idealized or materialized, built or demolished, meted out justice or exercised force, other worlds created cities, communities, men, or gods. The modern world debases. This is its specialty. . . . It debases the state; it debases man. It debases love; it debases woman. It debases the race, it debases the child. It debases the nation; it debases the family. It even debases . . . what is perhaps most difficult in the world to debase because this is something which has in itself, as in its texture, a particular kind of dignity, like a singular incapacity for degradation: it debases death."

There, taken quite at random, are attestations from Denmark

and France. And attestations to what? That the majority of men are trimmers. Which Dante could take for granted and go on. It is strange that there should be a generation, late in time, for which there is poetic news in the discovery that the world is a waste land. It always was, and the happy times for poets were when the fact was not surprising. It is as if we could be thrown into consternation by the announcement that each of our neighbors had two legs and needed food to live. The one great commonplace of morality, which is that most people are not moral at all—neither good nor bad—has ceased to be available. With it have ceased to be available such things as tragedy, comedy, irony, and the kind of indignation that can be sharp because it is final. The modern poet cannot end his plaint. His disgust grows monotonous. D. H. Lawrence races around the earth in search of a continent in which devils are indigenous, and angels common as air. He never arrives. So he never stops howling that the world is—what it is.

The problem is thought to be social, but it is theological. This does not mean that it is easily solved. Nor does it mean that those are wasting their time who work for the improvement of men's condition. Men are badly off, and simple justice could be farther spread; indeed it had better be, or mutual massacre will remove the race. The reformers are not wasting time. They are wasting eternity. The fraction is fixed: a very small numerator of those who are good or bad enough for poetry to be interested in, a very large denominator of those concerning whose existence poetry has no report to make. Poetry is fiercely moral, as to be sure Baudelaire was when he announced the agony of his *ennui*. But poetry is also, at any rate it was built to be, somehow the conqueror of time. It should pause as Pascal did to note that man's natural life is boredom, that time is endless and terrible; but it should only pause. The rest of the journey is through Hell and Heaven. The modern poet scarcely gets started on the long road, in the great subjects. This is because he shares the common delusion that Hell and Heaven are far away. They are here or nowhere, as Dante's unremitting relevance might prove. But we do not think they are. And in a sense we are right. We have lost the theology which placed them for us, and we have not found another which can place them again.

It may take thousands of years to find such a theology, to cut escape doors out of waste land which can take us into worlds whose footing is solid. When we escape now it is into oxygenless atmospheres and baseless wilds. Thousands of years. And meanwhile, what shall the poet do? A poet cannot make a theology; Blake tried and is incomprehensible, Hardy tried but only gave names to mist. Poets have to share a theology; and with many people. What then can the poet do in a world like ours which thinks that time, future time, will bring all things to clarity? Will see the little justice grow into the great justice? Will invert the fraction? Will sanctify the trimmers? Heaven only knows what he can do. He can refuse to be a fool in the infinite ways that foolishness is possible. But that is not enough for heaven. Or, in the long view, for poetry. Whether there is anything positive he can do is not for this note to determine.

# The Possible Importance of Poetry

POETRY desires to be interesting; or it should. By tradition it has a right to this desire, for there have been times when nothing was more interesting than poetry. If this is not such a time, the reason may be simply that we have lost our desire; or if not so, that we have lost touch with tradition. The present fact would seem to be that people do not consider poetry either interesting or important—two words for the same thing, and the people are the judge. So have they always been, in spite of every appeal to something beyond or above or beneath them. There is no appeal. It is to people that poetry must be interesting.

When they do not find it so, the fault conceivably is theirs: they have forgotten how to read. It is they, and not the poets, who have lost touch with tradition. But it is dangerous for poets at any time to make such a charge. In our time it is a plausible charge, for we can suspect, and indeed we are often told, that universal literacy has depressed literature. When the only aim is that everybody should be able to read something, no matter what, and when mass production of printed words has become the business of cynics who despise the very audience by which they profit, the outlook for distinguished thoughts and feelings would appear on the face of it to be poor. The contemporary poet, however, cannot afford to rest here. His job is what the job of poets has always been: to think and feel as deeply as he can, and to assume the existence of persons who will be glad that he has done so. And he had better assume that these are more than a few—ideally, he had better assume that they are all of us. He had better not count the number, at least beforehand; for if he does, he will end by limiting himself. "I am always made uneasy," Emerson wrote in his Journal, "when the conversation turns in my presence upon popular ignorance and the duty of adapting our public harangues and writings to the mind of the people. 'Tis all pedantry and ignorance. The people know as much and reason as well as we do. None so quick as they to discern brilliant genius or solid parts. And I observe that all those who use this cant most, are such as do not rise above mediocrity of understanding. . . . Remember that the hunger of people for truth is immense. The reason why they yawn is because you have it not."

Whenever poetry has been good it has had good subject matter—good for anybody, and it has not agonized about numbers. Today, I think, we do not hear enough about the subject matter of poetry. Criticism tends to ignore the question altogether. Poets are damned or praised for their way with language, as if language were the aim and end of all their art. Language is a lovely thing, and only human beings have it; but they have it, presumably, for something better still, and the greatest poets are those who have best understood this. There is no lord of language like Shakespeare; he could and did do everything with it; but what finally moves us as we read him or watch his plays is the knowledge he has of us, on a level deeper than words. We adore Shakespeare because he is wise, and because the world of men is given its right value in his works. It was for the same reason that the Greeks all but worshiped Homer, whom they knew by heart even though they knew nothing about the world of which he had written. The truth is, of course, that they did know his most important world, for it was the human world, and as such it was not different from theirs. Again they had in him a lord of language, but they noticed this less than they noticed how well he understood the passions, the ideas, and the absurdities of men. They watched Achilles learning what honor means; they watched Odysseus coming home; and they saw the soul of Hector reflected in the love of those around him—his family, his comrades, and his friends among the gods. By the same token, what is it that in modern times convinces a true reader of Dante that his reputation is deserved? His verbal cunning, and the peculiar fitness of his rhymes, his syntax? These of course; but at last it is the knowledge of the man, and the pity; the power of his feelings, the unwearied work of his thought, and the deep lake of his heart. Without these he would merely be ingenious, as without them Homer would be sound and fury, and Shakespeare an incessant bustling in the scenery.

But those three are the greatest poets, some may say: the very greatest; and what can we learn from them? They are too far removed, they are monsters of perfection, they are studied more than they are read, they are statues whose pedestals only may be approached. Nothing could be more mistaken. Yet it is the custom of our time. We do not believe that we can learn from the greatest things. They are not for us. Which is why so few discussions of poetry today, even among those who ought to know better, even mention the names of Shakespeare, Homer, and Dante; and why the poet is defined in terms that exclude those masters; and why the impression is abroad that it is somehow bad taste for poetry to be interesting to people. Subject matter is itself an embarrassing subject, from which quick refuge is sought in the techniques of rhythm and image, of caesura and ambiguity. Those things all have their fascination, but it is secondary to the further fascination of the art when ultimate demands are made upon it. The ultimate demand is that it be faithful to its ancient trust: that it treat of human truth, and more wisely and movingly than most men treat it even when they know, as ideally all men know, the content of such truth.

Poetry today means lyric poetry; it means the short poem; and that too can be a great thing, but it is not the greatest. It is as great as it can be when its author has wisdom and passion, and when it is clear that if there were an occasion he could convey his understanding in the more complex forms of narrative and drama. The Greeks never forgot that lyric poetry is but a third of poetry itself, and perhaps the least third. The big things are done in narrative and drama, for poetry's chief business is the business of story—of mankind in motion. Philosophy and science give us knowledge of men in the aggregate, or in essence; poetry commits individuals to action and follows them through careers. It conceives beginnings, middles, and ends, and is perhaps the only thing that can conceive them. Nature does not, and neither may philosophy or science; but poetry must. And it is the test of any poet—that is, of any storyteller—whether or not he can finish the story he has started. The beginning is fairly easy, as any young writer knows; even the middle sometimes charts its own course; but the end—for that, alas, experience and penetration are required. And in addition to those, a familiarity with the forms in which all human conduct finally manifests itself, the two forms of tragedy and comedy.

Tragedy and comedy are forms, not statements; or it may be that they are forms of statement. But any statement which they make is as far from platitude as the most sophisticated poet could desire. Poetry today despises platitude, and it is right in that. The pompous homilies, the "affirmations" and hymns of self-praise that pass in times like these as the sort of thing we ought to love in preference to the dim poetry we do on the whole have—I for one will take the dim poetry, since at least it is not hollow. But it must be clear that I would rather have something better than either of these. I would rather have story, and I would like to see it well grounded in the tragic and the comic visions which embrace all the knowledge we have yet accumulated concerning man's life.

Man's life is never good enough, and only men can know what this means. It means more than that the world of any given moment is a poor thing for even the best persons in it. Contemporary literature spends too much time, perhaps, and certainly too much effort, in proving by documentation that the twentieth century is not what some people thought it was going to be. What did they think it was going to be? An earthly paradise? Heaven itself? But if they thought this they were children, and poetry is not for children. Neither can it be written by children. It is the product of long seasoning and of bittersweet experience, neither of which things we have any right to expect in the very young. We do not think of Homer as very young; or Dante, or Shakespeare, or Sophocles, or Milton, or Hardy, or Yeats. Or Chaucer—who sounds in every verse he wrote as if he had been born with quizzical old eyes, and perhaps the small beard we cannot think of him without. The great poet knows the world, and how to live in it—also how not to live in it. He is not surprised because it has failed at being Heaven, or because most people in it fall grotesquely short of being angels. He seems to have expected this, and to have been prepared. The current notion of the poet as young, ignorant, helpless, and complaining is more recent than many of us think. Through most of human time the poet has been thought of in terms that suggest the old man of the tribe—the one who has lived longest and seen most, whose voice nevertheless has retained its original sweetness. Even in our day we have been witness to examples of this: Thomas Hardy, beginning to publish poetry at fifty-eight and ceasing only with his death at eighty-eight; William Butler Yeats, turning at middle age into the great poet he was at last to be; Robert Frost, unheard of by the world until he was nearing forty, and proceeding after that to become more himself with every advancing decade. We have these examples, and still we go on thinking of the poet as knowing less than we do—less, not more, which immemorially has been the assumption.

The poet knows how to live in the world and how not to live in it. That is to say, he locates the good life where it actually is—in the mind that can imagine and believe it. The mind of man not only sees worlds but creates them; and the worlds it creates are not here. This does not mean that they are illusory worlds, made up for solace and thin comfort. They are more substantial than the one we move through every day; but they are not here, and they cannot be verified by those who think this is the only world there is. Those who think that are either deceived or disillusioned, and chronically so. The poet is not deceived, for he has sharp eyes. But neither is he disillusioned, for in one very important sense he has never suffered from illusion. He has not thought that Heaven was in cities—or in the country, either, if that is what you think I mean. It is where it is, and only the mind can travel there. Shakespeare must have known contemporary England very well, but his mind traveled elsewhere in search of persons, stories, tragedies, comedies. It traveled to that region where all men's minds are at home, and it brought back news that made this world seem somehow a foreign place, as indeed it must always seem to the uncompromising imagination. It is the only place where we have addresses, but it is not where we chiefly live. Nor need we hate it because this is true. Dante, traveling also into Heaven and Hell, took his memories with him and used them there. Homer, dropping back several centuries in time, found heroes—which was what he wanted, and he knew he should not look for them in his next-door neighbors whom nevertheless he did not despise. They had not disappointed him, because he had never counted on them for more than they could deliver.

Poetry, in other words, takes it for granted that the world is not good enough for its best men. But all it can do with these men is to make them tragic or comic heroes—to show them as defeated by the very world to which they are superior. What if they succeeded? Poetry asks this question, asks it again and again, and at last decides that the answer is for no man to give. The poet is a man too, laughing and crying with other men. He certainly is not God. So he does not know the answer. But he knows the question, which he asks over and over in such a way as to suggest the extreme distinction of man's predicament. Man wants to change the world and cannot do so. The world will punish him if he tries, just as gravity will operate upon his body no matter how light he thinks it is. Hamlet is inconceivably brilliant, but he must die like any other man, and for the commonest reason—he has not survived his crisis. Don Quixote is the greatest gentleman we know, but the world cannot tolerate one who tries to teach it to be other than it is. The world is indeed a tough place. But what man could make it tender? No man, says poetry, no man at all, and sacrifices King Lear on the altar of the unchangeable. He learned, but learned too late. There is no appeal from the ways of the world, which must continue on its own terms or take us all down with it into chaos and confusion. Which does not mean that we should think it a nice thing. It is a terrible thing; or if not terrible, absurd. So tragedy and comedy say—and salvage out of the wreck the best ideas we have, the ideas that certain men could become heroes by expressing, even though they failed.

What if they had succeeded? The question is meaningless; or rather, we cannot imagine what it means, nor does the poet try. What if Socrates had succeeded in making all Athenians think well? What if Jesus had succeeded in making all Jerusalem over into the image of his Father? What if Don Quixote had persuaded all of Spain that knights were more real than merchants and monks? What if Hamlet had cleansed Denmark of its sin? What if Oedipus' finding of the truth had made him free? For one thing we should not now have the books of which these persons are the heroes. Or if we did have them, we could not believe them. We believe them because they falsify nothing in their report of the world. Their report of the human spirit—well, that is another matter. Neither do they falsify that by minimizing the dangers it must undergo, or by denying the supreme courage it inspires in those who properly possess it. The world is what it is, and the human spirit is what it is. And somehow they live together: ill-sorted companions, but the only companions there are for poetry to watch disappearing down the long perspective of life.

The possible importance of poetry is immense at any time. And why not now? I would make no exception of our time, though there are those who do. They are the ones who persist in identifying poetry with short poems, and who even then do not remember how great a short poem can be—for it can be dramatic too, and somehow narrative; it can imply careers, for ideas and for men. The short poem is better in those ages when the long poem is better; or, at the minimum, when it exists. The forms of literature reinforce one another, as tragedy and comedy do, which are the forms of thought. When fiction is good, then poetry can be good; and vice versa. Fiction indeed *is* poetry; or as I have put it here, poetry is story. This is not my idea, as you very well know; it is at least as old as Aristotle, and it has prevailed whenever poetry has been important to people.

But when I say fiction do I mean merely narratives or dramas in verse? Not necessarily. The ancient categories of lyric, epic, and dramatic poetry were not conceived in terms of verse alone, and it is fatal for us to suppose so. What we call prose fiction today is in fact the most interesting poetry we have; Aristotle would think so if he were alive, and he would be justified by the interest we show. Our movies, our westerns, our detective tales—he would wonder, perhaps, why so many of us failed to recognize those things too as contributions, however bad or good, to the poetry of this age. I have already spoken of Cervantes as if I thought he was the great poet of his age, along with Shakespeare his contemporary. That is exactly how I regard him, and I am not prevented from doing so by the fact that he wrote his greatest work in prose. He was a versifier too, but as such he does not interest us; whereas his vast poem called *Don Quixote* is among the glories of the world. Shakespeare wrote both verse and prose—sometimes, it would seem, indifferently, as if convenience alone dictated his choice; and his prose, unlike the verse of Cervantes, was itself a great thing, there being no better prose I think in English. But the question does not greatly matter. The vision was the thing in either case: the vision, and the knowledge that backed it up. The wisdom of these men is what makes them poets, as it is the wisdom of Tolstoy and Dostoievsky and Chekhov that makes us think of them, when we are serious, as Russia's poets. Is Dickens not a poet? Consider his passion and his joy as he contemplates humanity and sets it moving. The possible importance of poetry includes the chance that such men as these should continue to appear, and that we should have the generosity to recognize them as belonging to the highest class.

That we do not do so is perhaps the fault of our education, which keeps first things separate from one another. We study literature as if it were a thing by itself, and not only literature but English literature—even American literature, God save the mark. When American literature is good it is *literature*, as English or Greek literature is. And when *literature* is good it is a part of all we know. Not the only part, or even the best part, but certainly a part; and it is well that we should remember this. It is more likely to excel when the society that produces it considers neither it nor science, nor mathematics, nor philosophy, nor theology, nor medicine, nor law, nor mechanics, nor politics, nor economics, nor history, as the central subject matter of its thought. The central subject matter for any great age is life and truth; or perhaps it is justice and mercy. At any rate it is something that all arts and studies serve, and serve, we may suppose, equally. The Greeks were at one and the same time supreme in poetry, in philosophy, in science, and in mathematics. But this was not a coincidence, I suspect. They were great in each of these things because they were great in all the others, and because they thought that each of them testified to a vision which itself was the central thing. Their education, that is to say, was not specialized. All arts for them were finally one art, and the name of it was living well. Nor did they set the fine arts of poetry, painting, music, and sculpture above the practical arts and the intellectual (we should say liberal) arts. There was no hierarchy of importance among them, because there was none of them with which serious men could dispense. The carpenter made a house, the logician made a syllogism, and the poet made a poem. Each was doing what he could and therefore should, and nobody doubted the benefit.

We specialize, with the paradoxical result that no one knows for sure what it is that he is doing. Where there is no connection there can be no comparison. What is the difference, for instance, between the poet and the philosopher, or between the poet and the scientist? We do not state it well, because we do not think of all three men as artists. If they had that much resemblance in our minds, then they might have differences too, and we could measure these. We tend to assume that the differences are absolute; but this means in the end that they are absolutely small; or that the men themselves are. We often talk, as I have said, as if the poet were small. He might grow larger if he knew, or if we knew, what sphere he works in as distinguished from any other man; and if we thought of him as working in that sphere for our benefit; and if we thought of all men in their spheres as working in them for our good—our knowledge, our happiness, and our wisdom.

The poet has his subject matter as well as his skill; and his skill increases as he realizes what his subject matter is. If poetry has made any advances in our time—in, that is to say, the twentieth century—we should wonder what new subject matter it has found. I for one think it has made advances; but I am not in sympathy with those who say that these are merely technical. The concern, the conscious concern, has often been with devices of language and principles of diction. So was it in 1798, when Wordsworth called for poetry to adopt the language that men use. But Wordsworth had something to say in his new language; he needed the language, in fact, so that he *could* say what he thought and felt. The situation is no different now. With the new style of 1912—if that is the year from which we date a certain renaissance—there came new stuff; and I think the stuff explains the style. Wherever we look in that time we discover poets who themselves had discovered, or rediscovered, something worth saying in human speech. Irony returned, and the sense of tragedy; the sense of comedy, too, and even the sense of sin. Edgar Lee Masters dug up the Greek Anthology; Ezra Pound ransacked the older poetries of Europe and Asia; and Edwin Arlington Robinson attempted again the difficult art of story. T. S. Eliot experimented, to be sure, with stanzas and free verse; it is quite important that he did so; but it is still more important that he restored to poetry the stuff of theology, long absent and all but lost.

Robert Frost has rediscovered Job, whose wife says in *A Masque of Reason:*

> Job says there's no such thing as Earth's becoming
> An easier place for man to save his soul in.
> Except as a hard place to save his soul in,
> A trial ground where he can try himself
> And find out whether he is any good,
> It would be meaningless. It might as well
> Be Heaven at once and have it over with.*

There we have the accent we desire, and it is inseparable from the subject Frost has found. He found it where it waited for him, as the world waits for any man to recognize it. For any man, and for any poet. For there is nothing more important about a poet than that he is a man. He may not know more

* From *A Masque of Reason* by Robert Frost. Copyright 1945 by Robert Frost. By permission of Holt, Rinehart and Winston, Inc.

at last than all men do, but what he does know he knows well, and perfects himself in the art of expressing. What he knows, and what we know, is that the world is a hard place to live in at any cost, but that the cost is prohibitive only for those who make the mistake of thinking it is Heaven—or, worse yet, that it should have been.

# Leaves of Grass: 1855-1955

NOTHING about Walt Whitman is better known, or should be better known, than that in 1855 he sent an early copy of *Leaves of Grass* to Emerson in Concord and received in due course such a letter of thanks as any obscure poet in any age would almost have died to deserve. "I am not blind," said Whitman's master and the master of most writers in that day, "to the worth of the wonderful gift of *Leaves of Grass*. I find it the most extraordinary piece of wit and wisdom that America has yet contributed. I am very happy in reading it, as great power makes us happy. . . . I give you joy of your free and brave thought. I have great joy in it. I find incomparable things, said incomparably well, as they must be. . . . I greet you at the beginning of a great career."

The criticism of *Leaves of Grass* may be taken as starting here. Emerson was not specific; he cited no lines, no poems; and he said nothing of the subject matter concerning which Whitman had been witty and wise. If he remembered his own first book, *Nature*, published nineteen years before, he may have had in mind these sentences from its introduction: "We are now so far from the road to truth, that religious teachers dispute and hate each other, and speculative men are esteemed unsound and frivolous. But to a sound judgment, the most abstract truth is the most practical. Whenever a true theory appears, it will be its own evidence. Its test is, that it will explain all phenomena. Now many are thought not only unexplained but inexplicable; as language, sleep, madness, dreams, beasts, sex."

Our guess can be that Emerson saw in Whitman some sort of religious teacher, or at any rate a speculative man; that he felt in him the force of abstract truth; that he found him struggling with a true theory and with its evidences; that he suspected in this theory the power to explain all phenomena; and that he recognized here the very phenomena whose names he had spoken in 1836: language, sleep, madness, dreams, beasts, sex. For all of the six were important to Whitman, who indeed may have read the passage too, and even perhaps may have got it by heart. They are important phenomena at any time—now, certainly, no less than then—and only the most ambitious poets address themselves to them. We can be sure that Emerson admired Whitman's ambition; it was why he called him free and brave; and we may be nearly as sure that for him the ambition was enough. For Emerson, that is to say, there was little necessary difference between having great subjects for poems and being a great poet. And it is well to bear such a view in mind, because it is connected with the truth. But it is only connected; it is not the whole truth about poetry, which among other things is an art. Emerson had little patience with the art of poetry: a luxury he could afford, since now and then he was one of the finest of poets himself. If he was not so more often, the reason may have been this very indifference to art which meant that he could take ambition for success, or promise for accomplishment, as perhaps he did in the case of the stranger who had sent him *Leaves of Grass*, and certainly as most critics of that stranger have done throughout the ensuing century.

And still it is difficult to keep the distinction clear. Whitman himself never kept it clear; indeed, he did all he could to confuse it. He could never make up his mind as to how he wanted the world to consider him: whether as poet or as thinker, as artist or as prophet, as sayer or as seer. He saw the distinction well enough to be worried by it; he was uneasy about it until he died; but from the first—that is, from the time of the famous preface which Emerson undoubtedly read with the same excitement that it generates today—Whitman thought he must denounce those whose concern was with the art of poetry, or as he put it, with the "gaggery and gilt." Their concern, he said, was merely with devices to perfect "piano tunes." They were an effeminate crew, dainty and afraid. They did not know what he claimed to know, namely, that a great poet is neither more nor less than "the channel of thoughts and things without increase or diminution, and is the free channel of himself." The thoughts, the things, the poet's self—those are enough, he insisted; we shall not bother with detail, or craft, or criticism.

But criticism cannot be forever kept at bay. Nor at its best is it a trivial thing. It does to be sure assume that a poet is an artist, but so does time make this assumption—even more ruthlessly, for it is interested in nothing save success. A successful artist, says time, is one who knows how to do the thing he sets out to do, and knows how to do it so well that nothing, or at any rate the fewest possible things, can touch the result. Time has seen the death of many poets, and may be supposed to think, as criticism clearly does, that something must have been the matter with their work. It was not strong enough, or tough enough, or true enough, or simply good enough to resist the doubts men finally have that any book should be permitted to survive. Such doubts are sound, because we cannot have too many classics; the best must be indeed the best, beyond our power to deny it. A classic must stand at last alone: without apology, exegesis, or alibi. It must speak for itself to strangers; it must be intelligible, and seem true, after all its special friends are dead. It must have the minimum of weakness, vagueness, vanity, wind. It must be well made at the seams, to stand the long voyage it hopes to make, and to endure the waves either of contempt or of competition. It must have been made, in other words, by one who knew how to make such things, and nothing else about him will matter—who he was, how he looked, or what he thought about other things than the things he treated. Time and criticism ask no further questions, because no further questions are sensible. They are interested in nothing that is not sensible, and neither is any serious man.

Only two poets have weathered time and criticism without any loss whatever: Homer, still great and still popular after two and a half millenniums, and Shakespeare, still great and still popular after three and a half centuries. A few others come close to this distinction, but they have had their ups and downs of fame, their ins and outs of favor, and probably they will continue to do so. It is to Whitman's credit that he was never blind to Homer and Shakespeare; they were his heroes, and in a sense he had no others. In prose, in verse, he spoke of them constantly, either with simple reverence or with that more complicated respect which involves the recognition of rivals. For various reasons he refused to consider himself in competition with his contemporaries; but a sound instinct told him to beware of the great Greek and the great Englishman in whom he himself could find no fault—except, to be sure, that they had written for other times, which he vaguely called "feudal," and therefore were not for these times, which he vaguely called "modern." Even then he was disturbed by their close presence on Broadway and in public and private libraries. For they had survived without loss and were the best loved poets of these times as well as theirs. Who was more successful on the current stage than Shakespeare, and who but Homer still seemed, as Whitman knew he had always seemed, the very type of poet, the living model whom most if not all other poets merely approximated? Neither one of them, in spite of the fact that he had written for an age long dead, was dead himself. So all that Whitman could do when the rival's mood descended upon him was to reassert the difference he saw between the age of Agamemnon and the age of Jackson, or between the world of Hamlet and the world of Lincoln. This difference could be to him a very solid comfort; for he was the poet of the new world, and as such was beyond the reach of those august giants before the flood. Yet even then he had his nervous moments; the matter remained one that he must discuss; and the models were in his mind whenever he labored, as chronically he did, to enlarge, to reshape, to rearrange, to relabel the one book, *Leaves of Grass*, by which he expected his name to stand.

How long and how securely will it stand? That is the question which criticism at last must pose, and patiently wait for an answer. Thus far the answer has been slow in coming, and it may be that many further years must pass before it can state itself with confidence and clarity. Yet it is already time that we be as serious as we know how to be concerning the stature of Whitman's poetry; that we make of it the strictest demands, that we compare it with the greatest poetry, not the least, and that we pay no more attention than we please to the opinions of it held either by Whitman himself or by any of his numerous champions. For as everybody knows he had his champions; and he still has them—has, that is, critics in name only, persons who take the intention for the deed, the promise for the fulfillment, the ambition to be great for the fact of being great. These may be admirable persons, and indeed they are, but it is not their function to criticize; their function is to promote—a harmless function when recognized for what it is. Fortunately for criticism, they are fewer than they used to be. They are dying out with the times of which Whitman was so proud to be the spokesman. The middle of his century is less and less like the middle of ours. He thought his world was here to stay, but it has not stayed. Already, then, he is to some extent a period poet; not altogether so, of course, or else he would interest the historian more than he does the critic. And that is not the case. He is a living poet, and as such deserves all that criticism can do to him—or for him if you please. It can do much for him first and last. It can disembarrass him of irrelevant claims. It can separate the better from the worse among his poems; it can cut away the soft parts, it can leave the firm parts standing; it can say, or attempt to say, just what in him is good by any standard.

It was not for Emerson to apply standards in the angelic letter he sat down to write. If he saw Whitman as a philosophical poet, as pretty certainly he did, it was the philosophy that interested him most. He liked Whitman's ideas, which were not too different from his own, and which in any case were likable because they touched reality. Not only were they good ideas; they were good for the times; they were perhaps older than Whitman thought, but he had made them his own, and he had given them the airing they now needed. So did the times need airing; they would get that too, by virtue of this book. Emerson, rubbing his eyes, saw life in a volume of poems at last, and he did all that should have been expected of him when he said so in the way he did. Certainly he should not have been expected to judge this new philosophical poet *as a poet*, which is what has finally to be done. Nor does this mean anything so mechanical as judging the philosophy first and the poetry second. The two things are not that separable, assuming them to be separable at all. They are separable only to the extent that we can speak their names one after the other. But they operate at the same time in the same poem. The philosophy causes the poetry, and the poetry causes the philosophy, with the grand result that we feel and believe that we are in the presence of the truth, that the whole world is what the poet says it is, that he has explained, in Emerson's phrase, all phenomena; and not only explained them, but made them present and real, so that other or contrary things seem false or pale by comparison, and so that we who read are robbed, if only for the time being, of the power to imagine any other way of seeing, feeling, and comprehending the world we live in, and are proud to live in, with the poet.

Emerson of course did not have before him the bulky volume we now know as *Leaves of Grass*. Including the preface, there were only ninety-three pages, though they were large ones, in the book he read, and there were only twelve poems, all without titles. The first of the twelve, later to be called "Walt Whitman," and still later "Song of Myself," occupied more than half of the pages. It was and is one of Whitman's masterpieces, if not the chief one; it had the right position in the book, for it said most of what Whitman had to say, at least until 1865, and it said it altogether personally, drawing its authority from Whitman's innermost being insofar as he could be conscious of that being. Emerson needed no more than this magnificent poem, so candid yet so cryptic, so loose and yet so terse, so flowing yet so broken, as evidence of the author's wit and wisdom. It still is the key to *Leaves of Grass*, however reluctantly it sometimes turns in the lock. It is not systematic; it is perhaps a series of notes, or better yet a collection of inspired sayings; it is not cluttered with transitions, it does not seek to explain itself; it simply and confidently, if arrogantly too, is what it is, to be taken or left as the reader desires. Emerson took it, and then went on, we may suppose, to take such further masterpieces, minor only by comparison, as "The Sleepers," "I Sing the Body Electric," and "There Was a Child Went Forth."

It was an excellent selection, an exciting selection, from the poems Whitman had been writing since his thirtieth year or thereabouts: since the day when he cut himself loose from his own past and from what he took to be the past of the human race. We can envy Emerson the experience he had with a lean book that was mostly nerves and muscle. *Leaves of Grass* in its ultimate state is a greater book because it contains further masterpieces then unwritten. But in one vital respect it is less attractive. It is stuffed with repetitions of statements that once were fresher and did not need to be made again. Its author is afflicted with the modern disease of rewriting: he is always tinkering with his text—sometimes, granted, for the better, but sometimes not so. He cuts and he inserts; he regroups and rearranges; he improvises sections and provides transitions—dead connective tissue—between them. He composes "Inscriptions" which the reader shall find first, and at the end he keeps saying farewell to this same reader, bidding him take note and remember, assuring him of this or that meaning that he may not have expressed, hanging on for dear life to some image of his book as the rounded, systematic work which in fact it never was or could be, and indeed should never have tried to be. We do not require of a philosophical poet that he be systematic; we require only that he be always keen and convincing. Whitman dulls his final effect by laboring to convince us with something less than the best poetry he could write. For he is full of the notion that *Leaves of Grass* is a scripture, and that he is its editor as well as its maker. He is preserving it for posterity, he is altering it, coaxing it into shape, inserting things in it, taking things out, so that nothing will prevent its survival through the centuries ahead. Hence all the putty and the plastic wood. He is unwilling to let the individual poems stand free as their progenitors did in the original edition. It is as if he thought he had to keep on writing at a book he had not yet written, though in truth he had, for the best of his poems were that book. In his own words he was "garrulous to the very last"; and though we may love him for the admission, we are sorry that it has to be made.

It has to be made because Whitman, strangely enough for one whose first appearance was in the role of the supremely satisfied person—satisfied with himself and with every portion of his world—has come to be a person so tentative, so unsure, that he irritates and tantalizes rather than reassures us. He seems uneasy as to whether he has said what he wanted to say, or whether he knows now what that was. He slips away into hints and approximations, and above all into promises that he will say it yet, or that if he never does, others coming after him will. But so far, he sometimes confesses, his subject has eluded him; it is not in the book at all.

For it is not for what I have put into it that I have written this book,
Nor is it by reading it you will acquire it.

The subject, then, is over and above the book, which merely suggests it. Or the subject is himself, he is forced to say:

Before all my arrogant poems the real Me stands untouch'd, untold, altogether unreach'd,
Withdrawn far, mocking me with mock-congratulatory signs and bows,
With peals of distant ironical laughter at every word I have written.

The excuse he hopes he has, and keeps insisting he has, is the extreme difficulty of his assignment. Like Dante and Spenser he speaks of his book as a little bark that ventures in huge seas almost certain to overwhelm it. Like Milton he reaches after things yet unattempted in prose or rhyme. He must break new ground, and no wonder it is hard.

He remembers—or perhaps he does not remember—that the artist's business is nevertheless to find his subject and to finish the work which embodies it; to steer the bark into some port at last; to get there and make an end. He remembers—or perhaps he does not remember—that the great poet knows how to write his poem; he does not talk about the difficulty because he is occupied with conquering it; he does not promise to succeed tomorrow; he succeeds today. Homer did not discuss the problem of the epic; he wrote the *Iliad* and the *Odyssey*. Shakespeare did not write, at any rate in public, about whether or not it was possible to write *Hamlet;* he wrote it, and made it seem easy. But Whitman, after his brave start, is forever doubting that he knows where to go or what to do. Which indeed is strange, considering that start. And which is why, for all the fine poems his book contains, it is not the finished thing, the effective scripture, the moving whole he presumably once desired that it should be. Even his retouchings, his nudgings, his inscriptions and farewells, do not accomplish the result. For they are done half-heartedly, as if he knew they would not succeed.

The answer he gave himself, and in many a place gives us, is that *Leaves of Grass* is not a work of art at all. "This is no book," he says. "No one will get at my verses who insists upon viewing them as a literary performance, or attempt at such performance, or as aiming mainly toward art." *Leaves of Grass*, he seems to be saying, is so little like other books that perhaps it should be called something else. And if we ask again why it is that he expends so much effort in perfecting whatever he has between his hands, he says again that it is not a book as other books are books. If it is actually one, it is "a book separate, not link'd with the rest." Nor does it occur to him that this is a handicap rather than a help, since it means that he neither competes nor contributes, and so is lost, as it were, in literary space, with no masters for models, no company as he works. "The words of my book," he says, are "nothing, the drift of it everything." But in the long run, under the scrutiny of time and criticism, it is only the words that will count. The work of any poet is done with words. It is done with drift, too, but we must be the judges of that. And Whitman knew that this was so, or else he would not have denied it so vehemently. Somewhere in him was the consuming ambition of an artist. Somewhere in him too was the appalling suspicion that he had failed—not absolutely, in view of his masterpieces, but relatively to the vast vision of himself he once had had, and to the vaster vision he had had of the good world whose air he breathed.

He loved this world as a lover loves his mistress—loved all of it, including its alleged imperfections. It is a fine thing to be able to do this, and to talk about it in the intense, free way we associate with no one more than we do with him. But much of his talk is not intense, not free, and therefore, by his own criterion, not good. *Leaves of Grass* is more often than not relaxed and flabby; it is uncertain of itself; on many of its pages it is, frankly, a bore. And this could be not alone because Whitman paid too little attention to his art; it could be as well because his theory, his thinking, failed at times to be first-rate. A philosophical poet must have examined at some stage the grounds of his thought, and made them as firm as possible. He has to be more than a thinker, but he had better think. He will always have a problem, of course, since that is the fate of philosophers. And Whitman's problem was an immemorial one: if the universe is to be accepted in all of its parts, if every part of it is to be loved and praised, how can one avoid monotony and unreality, how can one say more than the simple word *Yes?* For most men find the world both good and bad; they like some parts of it better than others, even when they don't know why. And this is likely to be true even of men like Whitman who do not want it to be true. For Whitman, as for Lucretius, all things were natural; and at least for Whitman all things were good. How then could he disapprove of anything—for instance, the piano poet, or the fool who corrupts, degrades, and defiles his body? Whitman regularly denounces this poet and this fool, and does so in the face of his insistence at other times that he accepts everything and everyone. But then he realizes what he has done, and makes amends by listing all the objects in the world for which he feels affection. Hence his famous catalogues which no one can read through. Every river makes the grade, every trade and occupation, every city, every valley, every individual, every class, every thought, every mountain, every man. Somehow the review is not impressive; it can even be ludicrous, with its suggestion that if Whitman had not come along to love these things they would have felt neglected. He has a special license to approve of you and me, of democracy and sin, of India and Christ. It is a jumble before he has finished.

He embraces too much; he stretches himself thin; he becomes breathless with adoration. He sounds as if he were exaggerating—in art, a fatal weakness. Nor does he sound at these moments like one possessed, and therefore in some degree to be condoned. He makes his catalogues in cold blood; his theory tells him to. So there could be something wrong with the theory, or else with the thinker who holds it. And this could be summed up in his own phrase: "There is no evil." An artist, or at any rate a literary artist, is seriously handicapped if he has no theory of evil; for then his vision of good lacks definition; he does not know why he likes it. It is natural to love the good, but before that it is necessary to know how to recognize it, and to guess what its price is—or better yet, its pricelessness, which experience of evil defines. The vision of good which does not start from a sense of evil will be a watery vision, colorless and shapeless, indistinct and finally depressing. Whitman's vision of the good is at its best a sharp and wonderful thing; at its worst it is unconvincing because it lacks lines to limit it, and consequently lacks form. It is an ample vision, and for that it is to be admired, just as Whitman is to be admired for his all-but-incredible refusal ever to judge. He is like Christ in this, except that he has no such reason as Christ had, and incidentally no such capacity for anger in the presence of evil. The figure of Christ is always clear and firm; Whitman's figure is wavering, and sometimes it is timid—because he does not know what he thinks. He does not follow his thought even as far as Lucretius followed his; he is by no means so ruthless, so possessed, so on fire. Lucretius, with bad logic, denounced religion; if everything is a part of nature, then religion is too; but religion was in his way and he said so with his whole might. Whitman, who had his own religion, accepted all others too, though most of them were in his way. He was not sure he shouldn't. He was not sure of most things. He did not see his vision to the end.

This may have been why he played as he did with the notion of himself in the role of orator. "A Song of Joys" inevitably gets around to the subject:

O the orator's joys!
To inflate the chest, to roll the thunder of the voice out from
the ribs and throat,
To make the people rage, weep, hate, desire, with yourself,
To lead America—to quell America with a great tongue.

Memorandums survive which show that he studied the techniques of the platform, and hungered for success upon it. And it has been supposed that it was good for his poetry to do so; whereas it was surely bad, since it made his poetry exclamatory, gesticulative, hyperbolic, and loud. The art of oratory as he understood it was the art of saying very little with vast force. Socrates suggested more than once that when understood most deeply it is like any other art: its function is to tell the truth. The arts of oratory and poetry are not enemies of each other when both of them are understood to have this function. But Whitman's ideal orator was all voice, all ribs and throat, all personality; and that has nothing to do with poetry, which does its work with a deadly stillness, marshaling words somewhere behind the scenes and sending them forth when it is time for them to come. The poet makes his words do his work, and hopes that they will seem to be doing only their own. Whitman himself could get good work out of his words, though not in such a passage as this from "Song of the Open Road":

Forever alive, forever forward,
Stately, solemn, sad, withdrawn, baffled, mad, turbulent, feeble,
dissatisfied,
Desperate, proud, fond, sick, accepted by men, rejected by men,
They go! they go! I know that they go, but I know not where
they go,
But I know that they go toward the best—toward something great.

It would be difficult to find in any poet a series of lines more forced and hollow than these. And the reason is that Whitman does not believe what he says; he simply could not, if he is the man who wrote "Song of Myself" or "The Sleepers," in neither of which is anybody going anywhere, least of all forward. *Go* and *forward* sound like cant words, and so they lack the force that the words of poetry should have.

The words of poetry can do with stillness for a subject—as when in "The Sleepers" Whitman hovers over all the prone people on earth and gazes down at them raptly, motionlessly, while the night itself stands fixed and watches with him. So in "Song of Myself" he is being what he is, and saying so; he is going nowhere, there is no forward or backward, there is only the present moment, here, with him the solitary figure, "gross, mystical, nude," somewhere near its center, contemplating himself. The great poet does not ask where the world is going or where it should go; he considers what it is in its own quiet essence, year after year and age after age, now no less than then, and there no more than here. The mystic—and Whitman at his best was that—is stricken where he stands, ecstatic over what he sees; and he refrains from moving lest the thing he looks at be startled and depart. Nor is it always easy to comprehend what he murmurs while he gazes. He is not saying it for us merely, though it is also true that he is not talking in his sleep. The obscurity of certain stretches in "Song of Myself," not to speak of "The Sleepers" again, is almost absolutely dense. An example would be the description of the speaker's senses, particularly his sense of touch, which must have been an extraordinary thing, comprehensible perhaps only to psychologists. But this obscurity is preferable to the hollowness of the "forward" passage in "Song of the Open Road." In the first case he was being a prophet, in the second he was trying to sound like one; he was saying what he thought he ought to say about "the progress of the souls of men and women along the grand roads of the universe." In what he called his "native moments" he did not bother with such nonsense. The soul, he knew, goes nowhere. It simply is. And it is Whitman's distinction that he belongs in the company of those who have suddenly seen, felt, heard that this is so.

The experience was mystical, which is to say that its truth did not have to be proved. It was its own evidence, as Emerson said. Whitman remarked in "Song of the Answerer" that "The words of true poems do not merely please." Not merely, no; but our pleasure is one of their aims, and in Whitman's best poems—or, if you like, his true poems—the words please instantly, at the same time that they suggest all sorts of things the reader will have to think about before he is through. But they do please; they are natural; they are memorable—they give us the impression that just as they had never been used this way before, so they will never need to be used this way again. Their authority is simple and immediate, their power is felt like a presence, and so, to quote Emerson once more, they make us happy. That is to say, they are successful words in successful poems, which compete with other successful poems in the world and hold their own.

Whitman's sense of such competition was more lively than he liked to admit. Sometimes he denied it altogether, as we know. He thought of himself as having been placed beyond comparison with the great poets of the past by being born just when and where he was. But he could also remember his peers, and as he did so he could wonder whether he had been wise in cutting loose from their company. He had repudiated, for example, meter; he invented a long, loose line which would leave him free to fill it with whatever belonged there, whether this was little or much. He knew of course that Homer and Shakespeare had not been slaves to meter; in their hexameters and blank verse they were conspicuously free, for they were able to say anything at all in the precise way it should be said. A master of meter is not a slave for the simple reason that he *is* a master. The poets of Whitman's day whom he rightly despised were masters of nothing, and least of all their verse, which lacked energy as most verse does in most generations. Whitman, however, did not propose to restore the energy that had been lost—or never, it may be, even imagined; instead he abandoned the form, and loafed in the long line he preferred instead. The result is sometimes wonderful and sometimes woeful. But we are in no position to guess what he would have done within the form he turned his back on; he never mastered it, even in contempt. His stricter poems—"Eidólons," for example, and "Pioneers! O Pioneers!"—are monotonous and grinding; they do not truly move; or else like "O Captain! My Captain!" they are singsong. The author of "When Lilacs Last in the Dooryard Bloom'd," using the loose line for the same subject, did infinitely better. In such a masterpiece the poet is clearly in charge of his own form; and this was true of Whitman often enough so that we must say his own form is justified.

There is only one dimension it lacks in his hands. He cannot be humorous with it. He can be witty, as Emerson pointed out, but he cannot be humorous in the way Carl Sandburg his disciple has been. There is Sandburg's fish-crier on Maxwell Street in Chicago:

> His face is that of a man terribly glad to be selling fish, terribly glad that God made fish, and customers to whom he may call his wares from a pushcart.

Or there is the famous question:

> Tell me why a hearse horse snickers hauling a lawyer's bones.

Or there is "Bas-Relief":

> Five geese deploy mysteriously.
> Onward proudly with flagstaffs,
> Hearses with silver bugles,
> Bushels of plum-blossoms dropping
> For ten mystic web-feet—
> Each his own drum-major,
> Each charged with the honor
> Of the ancient goose nation,
> Each with a nose-length surpassing
> The nose-length of rival nations,
> Somberly, slowly, unimpeachably,
> Five geese deploy mysteriously.

Whitman could do nothing like that, having in fact no sense of humor. It is a genuine defect in a poet, though some great ones have survived it, and he did.

"Sing me the universal," said Whitman to his muse, and there was something humorless in the injunction. Particular things are the stuff of poetry. The greater the poem the more universal we are willing to call it, but what interested us in it was the single thing with which it dealt, and which it managed to make real. Reality is of course a universal term, and the great poet knows where he stands with respect to it. The great poet was once, and still is in some deep part of himself, a philosopher. In his capacity as poet, however, he has disciplined himself to deal, or seem to deal, with nothing whatever save things that can be seen, with individual things whose surface truth he is content to render, leaving us, the beholders of these individual things, as free as men ever are to judge and interpret their companions in creation. The true poem has a limited subject—or shall we say a limited object—to which the poet gives his unlimited powers, remaining with it, rendering it with strict fidelity, until there is no more of it that can be shown. Until, for example, Hector is buried; or until Hamlet, having said all he could say, observes that the rest is silence.

In his best poems Whitman remembers this. His worst ones are those he forced himself to write in the absence of such knowledge. Indeed, the trouble with *Leaves of Grass* as a whole book, a book that tries to be round and complete, is precisely that it has an unlimited subject, and has it all the time that it is conscious of itself. It strains to swallow the camel, not the gnat. Its author says:

I will not make poems with reference to parts,
But I will make poems, songs, thoughts, with reference to ensemble,
And I will not sing with reference to a day, but with reference to all days.

The program is not agreeable, and we yawn. We expect poets to take the parts, not the ensemble: as many parts as they have years to treat, and one at a time. Of Shakespeare we finally say, and so did Whitman say, that his knowledge of men was comprehensive, even universal; but play by play we have noted that he gave himself entirely to its characters and to no others under the sun. And if we say of Shakespeare too that he had a wonderful power to accept and love all kinds of persons, good and evil, brilliant and stupid, we say this only after the entire population of his poems has passed in review. While they were passing Shakespeare said nothing of this; he merely let them speak; it is we who think universal thoughts as a grand result of the specific lives we have seen lived, the specific deaths we have seen deserved or not deserved. Whitman, claiming as he does in many of his poems that his subject is all things and all men, and suggesting as he makes the claim that if anything else were true he would be a trivial fellow, takes a short cut to the universal which will not in fact bring him there. It will bring him rather to the deserts of listed things with which we grow impatient because there seems to be no reason why they should be of one size rather than another. The lists seem endless because Whitman cannot end them; there is no principle by which he could, just as there is no principle by which we could recognize that the end was reached. These are the pages we skip, willing to grant a few examples but staggered by the hundreds we are given. In the preface to the first edition, the preface Emerson read, tribute is paid to "the solid and beautiful forms of the future where there are now no solid forms." Solid form—Whitman on the whole does not have it because his theory, such as it was, made it impossible. If all things are equal in truth, beauty, and goodness, then no one thing is ever especially good, beautiful, or true. Without a hierarchy of goods, nothing in fact will be either good or bad, and no subject for a poem will exist. Or at any rate no subject for a book of poems which is trying to be one poem in the large. Nothing will be possible except catalogues of this or that. And so we get the catalogues, as broad as they are long and as shallow as they are broad. Whitman, sticking stubbornly to his theory, has no way to focus his or our attention upon one object, one person, within whose outline all the meaning of the world may secretly and unobstrusively exist. The outline is the thing, and Whitman cannot draw it.

Most of the time, that is, he cannot. In his good poems he can and does, and that is why they are good poems. Indeed they are great poems because their outlines are so very sharp and because these outlines are filled in with everything they should contain—everything we had desired, and much, much more than that; for any great poet surprises us with what he knows, and takes us deeper into the territory of his theme than we could have imagined going. Also, Whitman's power of phrasing is constant here—not intermittent, not accidental, as it was in the ambitious but unsuccessful works with which *Leaves of Grass* is unfortunately so full, but ever-present and ever-pleasing, not to say ever deeply moving. The rhythm is now organic; the length of any line justifies itself; the beat of the music corresponds, we feel, to the beat of the writer's mind and pulse; and instead of poems which easily could be shorter or longer we have poems whose size is right for the subject, and whose energy drives them at the proper moment toward genuine conclusions. These great poems, though lyric in their genius, have beginnings, middles, and ends. Aristotle said that long poems should have those three parts, and it is one of the wisest things ever said; but it is true for short poems too, since short poems, if they aim to be powerful, must have their own dramatic tides, they must aim for some shore and reach it.

No reader of *Leaves of Grass* fails to find and to love for himself—almost as if a secret were being shared between him and the author—a number of very short poems which have the air of being notes, say, or sketches. For the most part they are descriptions of things Whitman has just seen, ideas that have just struck him, or memories miraculously just come back out of a past he had forgotten. Or so they seem, whatever may be the facts about their composition. We do not know such facts, nor does it matter; we have the individual object or idea—it may, actually, be only a state of mind or an excitement along some nerve—before us in its natural form, intensely rendered for us but at no point swollen or deformed by the exaggeration to which Whitman at other moments was addicted. The stuff of these pieces is highly particular, though it is familiar to us too, or we can imagine that it is. Sometimes they are imbedded as it were in longer poems, they are single lines, with little or no context before or after, that leap out and ring in our ears. Such a line is this one from "Song of the Open Road":

> Why are there trees I never walk under but large and melodious
> thoughts descend upon me?

For the most part, however, they stand alone, with titles, and beckon us to read them as we pass. "A Farm Picture" is three lines:

> Through the ample open door of the peaceful country barn,
> A sunlit pasture field with cattle and horses feeding,
> And haze and vista, and the far horizon fading away.

"The Runner" is four lines:

> On a flat road runs the well-train'd runner,
> He is lean and sinewy with muscular legs,
> He is thinly clothed, he leans forward as he runs,
> With lightly closed fists and arms partially rais'd.

And "Beautiful Women," which Rembrandt might have written, and somehow did with his etcher's tools, is only two lines:

> Women sit or move to and fro, some old, some young,
> The young are beautiful—but the old are more beautiful than the young.

Others of course are a little longer, though not very long, and never at all too long. "The World below the Brine" penetrates the depths of the sea, peoples the darkness there with animals and plants, then emerges into our upper world again, remarking upon its difference from the one just left, and remarking too upon the host of further worlds concerning which we know as little as whales and sea-leopards, lichens and sea-lettuces, know concerning us; and it does this in eleven lines. "The Dalliance of the Eagles" reports a "sudden muffled sound," "the rushing amorous contact high in space together" of "four beating wings, two beaks," in ten lines no word of which is out of place or pace. "The Torch" is briefer, as it should be because so little is seen; but it is well seen:

> On my Northwest coast in the middle of the night a fisherman's group stands watching,
> Out on the lake that expands before them, others are spearing salmon,
> The canoe, a dim shadowy thing, moves across the black water,
> Bearing a torch ablaze at the prow.

"The Ox-Tamer" is of ampler scope because the man in it, "my farmer friend," "my silent, illiterate friend," has tamed a hundred oxen, and they are in the poem. Note that in each of these poems there is a single thing, or a single set of things, which focuses the poet's effort. "On the Beach at Midnight" has the entire sky in it, but only as seen by a man and a boy;

and because we see through their eyes we see exactly what Whitman wants us to see:

> Amid a transparent clear belt of ether yet left in the east,
> Ascends large and calm the lord-star Jupiter,
> And nigh at hand, only a very little above,
> Swim the delicate sisters, the Pleiades.

These are the great *little* poems of Whitman; and some of them are greater still because they are more than descriptions of external things, they are resolutions or interpretations of them, they make applications of them in the life of the speaker, as of course in the life of the listener too. There is, for example, the famous spider:

> A noiseless patient spider,
> I mark'd where on a little promontory it stood isolated,
> Mark'd how to explore the vacant vast surrounding,
> It launch'd forth filament, filament, filament, out of itself,
> Ever unreeling them, ever tirelessly speeding them.
>
> And you O my soul where you stand,
> Surrounded, detached, in measureless oceans of space,
> Ceaselessly musing, venturing, throwing, seeking the spheres to connect them,
> Till the bridge you will need be form'd, till the ductile anchor hold,
> Till the gossamer thread you fling catch somewhere, O my soul.

There is the equally famous Southern tree:

> I saw in Louisiana a live-oak growing,
> All alone stood it and the moss hung down from the branches,
> Without any companion it grew there uttering joyous leaves of dark green. . . .

And there is the picture of Whitman himself as he watches a world he cannot change, and makes no move to change:

> I sit and look out upon all the sorrows of the world, and upon all its oppression and shame,
> I hear secret convulsive sobs from young men at anguish with themselves, remorseful after deeds done,

I see in low life the mother misused by her children, dying, neglected, gaunt, desperate,
I see the wife abused by her husband, I see the treacherous seducer of young women,
I mark the ranklings of jealousy and unrequited love attempted to be hid, I see these sights on the earth,
I see the workings of battle, pestilence, tyranny, I see martyrs and prisoners,
I observe a famine at sea, I observe the sailors casting lots who shall be kill'd to preserve the lives of the rest,
I observe the slights and degradations cast by arrogant persons upon laborers, the poor, and upon negroes, and the like;
All these—all the meanness and agony without end I sitting look out upon,
See, hear, and am silent.

That is a catalogue, but for once Whitman knows why he makes it, just as he knows how to render, by it and other means, the sense he has of being suspended, powerless, staring at a world in which almost everything is bad but in which, so far as he himself is concerned, there is no possibility of improvement. This is how, with tensions such as we are moved by here, poetry accepts the universe. It does not talk of doing it; it does not promise to do it; it does it, now, in this present moment which has the feel of eternity and the face of authentic circumstance.

Two outstanding sections of *Leaves of Grass*, "Calamus" and "Drum-Taps," throng with such brief masterpieces. The "Calamus" poems are impressive by their very silence and shyness—Whitman whispers of the men he loves, and cannot be doubted as he assures us that in these whispers his most intimate, most honest voice is speaking. The vignettes of battlefields in "Drum-Taps" are silent too, somewhat as Brady's photographs are silent; they are time exposures, delicate and just in every detail, and unforgettable in the way that our own most fugitive, most vivid memories can be unforgettable, for reasons we shall never know. There is greater length and there is more action in "Come Up from the Fields Father," but it too is strangely stationary in its perfect, single stillness: a family gathers to read a letter about the wounding of its son, and about his death if they but knew that it had happened. Only we and Whitman know that it has happened.

One of the "Calamus" poems puts a question—or makes a statement, for it is a rhetorical question—of the utmost importance to Whitman. "What indeed is finally beautiful except death and love?" His indubitable masterpieces, his extended and massive ones, build themselves on this foundation. The first of them, and they are three, does not rest squarely upon it because it had not then been laid. "Song of Myself" is more interested in life than it is in either death or love; it celebrates the poet's discovery of his own life—of its outline, of its content, of its structure, of its color and inward form, of its eccentricity that yet is central to the life of man, of its strangeness which nevertheless must be lived with and adored because while it is strangeness it is also truth—and the celebration takes for the most part the form of argument; or if not argument precisely, then epigram and paradox. But implicit even here is the further discovery, to be announced at least as early as the second edition of 1856, in a poem then called "Poem of Wonder at the Resurrection of the Wheat" but now known as "This Compost," that life and death do not separate themselves in the imagination, that in some miraculous way they are one subject, one thing; and that if either one of them is pre-eminent for poetry it is death, since death is the limiting, the framing force, the beginning and ending act out of which the middle derives its meaning. Whitman, that is to say, had made the discovery that only great poets make: the supreme subject is death. Little poets may think they have made it, but all they become as a result is maudlin or morbid. Great poets rise through it to reality and power; life is still their theme, but death is their language, death is their symbol and motive force; only through death may life be understood. Death transforms itself for them into a living thing. It has positive dignity and beauty, to be accepted for the same reason that life is to be accepted, and on the whole to be accepted first.

The second of Whitman's masterpieces in the major mode came three years after "This Compost," in 1859. Published the next year in *Leaves of Grass* as "A Word Out of the Sea," it was subsequently reworked and much improved—this is one case where Whitman rewrote with excellent results—and given the title by which we now know it: "Out of the Cradle Endlessly Rocking." It is lyric, not argument; it is one protracted, impassioned song in celebration of death. It is narrative as well; it is a reminiscence, somewhat in the spirit of Wordsworth's "Prelude," which reconstructs one moment in the poet's life when he was a boy by the seashore. *One* moment, we note; and we note too that in the first line we are given the sea, which can be thought of as a grave, as also a cradle—death and life together. In some briers by the shore there had been two birds, "two feather'd guests from Alabama," alternately sitting on the eggs in their nest, one watching, "silent, with bright eyes," while the other flew out over the waves and then returned. But once the female did not return; hour after hour, day after day, she did not return. And so the boy listened as the solitary he-bird broke his heart in song.

O night! do I not see my love fluttering out there among the
breakers?
What is that little black thing I see there in the white?

High and clear I shoot my voice over the waves,
Surely you must know who is here, is here,
You must know who I am, my love.

O past! O happy life! O songs of joy!
In the air, in the woods, over fields,
Loved! loved! loved! loved! loved!
But my mate no more, no more with me!
We two together no more.

Then the boy's heart would have broken too had he not implored the sea to send him the meaning of what he had seen and heard, and had not "the savage old mother incessantly crying" consented.

Whereto answering, the sea,
Delaying not, hurrying not,
Whisper'd me through the night, and very plainly before day-
break,
Lisp'd to me the low and delicious word death,
And again death, death, death, death,

Hissing melodious, neither like the bird nor like my arous'd child's
heart,
But edging near as privately for me rustling at my feet,
Creeping thence steadily up to my ears and laving me softly all
over,
Death, death, death, death, death.

Which I do not forget,
But fuse the song of my dusky demon and brother,
That he sang to me in the moonlight on Paumanok's gray beach,
With the thousand responsive songs at random,
My own songs awak'd from that hour,
And with them the key, the word up from the waves,
The word of the sweetest song and all songs,
That strong and delicious word which, creeping to my feet,
(Or like some old crone rocking the cradle, swathed in sweet
garments, bending aside,)
The sea whisper'd me.

"My own songs awak'd from that hour." The discovery of death made Whitman a poet, and this is the way he tells us. Poetry could hardly be better, and very seldom is. "Out of the Cradle Endlessly Rocking" is not merely one of his masterpieces; it is one of *the* masterpieces, and alone would justify the reputation of its writer.

He was better only once: in the dirge for Lincoln, "When Lilacs Last in the Dooryard Bloom'd." The Civil War, just ended with Lincoln's life, had been not so much the making as the remaking of the great poet who slept in Whitman's bones. Death now had become tragic and particular: the deaths of soldiers, the death of America as Whitman had known it in the days of Eden, the days of the Children of Adam; and now the death of "the sweetest, wisest soul of all my days and lands." The greatest man in Whitman's world had died, a man not himself, a man quite outside himself; and that was an advantage too for the poet who was to begin his crowning piece, for the subject matter of poetry should be outside, must be outside, if one is to go and put oneself in it. Whitman went to the subject of Lincoln with good and evil defined in his imagination, with each of those great things limited and made lifelike by the other. And he bore with him a set of symbols which to the accompaniment of magnificent music he could weave and intertwine as plastic artists do their visible, their tangible materials. The lilac, the star, the bird are concrete, irreducible images; the poem organizes itself around them as if by a natural process, though it is of course the artistic process at its best. Whitman is there too; "Lilac and star and bird" are "twined with the chant of my soul." The importance of the subject is finally in the understanding Whitman has of it. But it is something to be understood; and once more the song of a bird assists the musician of the spirit to find his voice: once more there is a great hymn to death:

> Come lovely and soothing death,
> Undulate round the world, serenely arriving, arriving,
> In the day, in the night, to all, to each,
> Sooner or later delicate death.
>
> Prais'd be the fathomless universe,
> For life and joy, and for objects and knowledge curious,
> And for love, sweet love—but praise! praise! praise!
> For the sure-enwinding arms of cool-enfolding death.

There is the summit of *Leaves of Grass*. It has other eminences, and on the lower ground there are foothills—the great little poems—which time will find it hard to wash away. Time and criticism. Already they have eroded the mountain, as is the way with all such things—a good way, since it leaves what ought to be left, and shows it in interesting shapes. Probably they will cut still deeper in. But certain rocks will endure as granite does. That, at this moment in time, is criticism's guess.

# The Poems of Thomas Hardy

A TEXT for any discussion of Thomas Hardy's poems might be the 373rd pensée of Pascal: "I shall here write my thoughts without order, and not perhaps in unintentional confusion; that is true order, which will always indicate my object by its very disorder. I should do too much honor to my subject if I treated it with order, since I want to show that it is incapable of it." Pascal's subject, to be sure, was not anybody's poems; it was everybody's life, it was the whole of experience as he tried to grasp it. Yet the text has a peculiar fitness in Hardy's case, for it can be made to refer not merely to the overwhelming volume and variety of his poetic output but to the view he himself took of the world; or the views, for there were many of these, and he never pretended that they were consistent with one another.

In one of his prefaces he confessed how difficult it had been to arrange the present poems in anything like a natural or rational order. Indeed, it was impossible, and so he had given up. "I mean," he said, "the chance little shocks that may be caused . . . by the juxtaposition of unrelated, even discordant, effusions; poems perhaps years apart in the making, yet facing each other. . . . But the difficulties of arranging the themes in a graduated kinship of moods would have been so great that irrelation was almost unavoidable with efforts so diverse. I must trust for right note-catching to those finely-touched spirits who can divine without half a whisper, whose intuitiveness is proof against all the accidents of inconsequence." The problem, familiar of course to any poet, must have been particularly torturous for Hardy, who had been prolific for so long. The eight volumes of short poems he published between 1898 and 1928—between, that is, his fifty-eighth and his eighty-eighth years—contained by no means all new matter. He was always bringing forward poems he had written in the 1860's, or in any of the three subsequent decades; for he started as a poet, and only because he could not get published in that capacity had he written novels. Now that he was determined to be known as a poet and nothing but a poet he ransacked his desk for "effusions" that might still do. No wonder he found it difficult to arrange the result.

The modern reader cannot do so either; nor can the modern critic decide with readiness which poems of Hardy's are the best, let alone the most characteristic. No poet more stubbornly resists selection. And this has not been to Hardy's advantage in the field where reputations are made. There is no core of pieces, no inner set of classic or perfect poems, which would prove his rank. Perhaps no poem of Hardy's is perfect; indeed, there is no great poet in whom imperfection is easier to find. Yet he is a great poet, and there are those who love him without limit even though they will admit his thousand failures and defects. With such persons it is the whole of him that registers and counts; one thing they would be reluctant to admit, namely, that out of his *Collected Poems* a *Selected Poems* might be put together which would contain everything pertaining to his essence. His essence, they would insist, is everywhere in the body of his work: in the capillaries, the tissues, no less than in the sinews and the heart. For them, in other words, the *Collected Poems* is neither too long nor too miscellaneous; its reputation with them depends upon the very richness that puts other readers off. They have made the effort the volume requires, and the reward of that effort is their knowledge of a poet who is great even when he is not writing well. He is great in himself, as one who thinks, feels, sees, and speaks; and he cannot lose their allegiance.

This miracle is worked in the *Collected Poems* alone; not in the slight verse play, *The Famous Tragedy of the Queen of*

*Cornwall*, or even in that more impressive drama in one hundred and thirty scenes, *The Dynasts*. It is good to have read *The Dynasts* once, for it contains curious and wonderful things; but few can have read it twice, at least all the way through. It does not get close to its people, whom Hardy too convincingly calls automata, cheese-mites, and mackerel. The view he takes of them is from too far away. This of course is the view he wants to take, since a theory rules him as he writes: a theory not unlike that of Tolstoy as he wrote *War and Peace* on the same subject, the wars of Napoleon. For neither man did individuals count, at any rate so far as theory went: there was no such thing as character or will, there was only mass movement, and even in this movement there was no meaning. But Tolstoy so far forgot his theory as to create Natasha, Andrey, and Pierre, to name only three out of dozens of souls to whom his pen gave life; whereas Hardy, with that stubbornness which his admirers will always forgive him, refused to budge from the platform he had erected whereon to stand and state his thesis—the calamity of Napoleon was fortuitous, without design or moral, nor were the sufferings of innumerable men so much as noted by the Immanent Will whose unfeeling mind worked

> unconsciously, as heretofore,
> Eternal artistries in Circumstance.

The Spirits with whom Hardy shares his platform, bodiless beings who have no more control over the drama than he has, say magnificent things in a monotone their poet never violates; but they say what he chooses to have them say, since they are nothing but spokesmen for his metaphysics. When we descend into the action—battles, conferences, love passages, riots, and duels—we do not find ourselves among people to whom warmth has even by inadvertence been given. Nor do these people speak fine verse, as often the Spirits do; they are not enough alive for that, nor does Hardy wish them to be. He has been more eloquent in his stage-directions; it is to those that the reader is most likely to return. For example, this early one:

> The nether sky opens, and Europe is disclosed as a prone and emaciated figure, the Alps shaping like a backbone, and the branching mountain-chains like ribs, the peninsular plateau of Spain forming a head. Broad and lengthy lowlands stretch from the north of France across Russia like a grey-green garment hemmed by the Ural mountains and the glistening Arctic Ocean.
>
> The point of view then sinks downward through space, and draws near to the surface of the perturbed countries, where the peoples, distressed by events which they did not cause, are seen writhing, heaving, and vibrating in their various cities and nationalities.

That is eloquent, surely; indeed, it is brilliant; but it closes a door on drama which is something like the door of a tomb. Those of us who insist on entering must abandon all hope of making human sense out of what we see.

No, it is the *Collected Poems* upon which Hardy's reputation will be obliged to rest. And this is a volume, as has already been hinted, in which a traveler can lose his way. Its contents are a cavern the quality of whose darkness is always changing, and the number of whose recesses appears to increase as the explorer stumbles on. Lights gleam and then subside, only to be lit again in further corners. The reader, that is to say, is forever making new discoveries: either of Hardy or of himself. If of Hardy, they have to do with dimensions of his thought and feeling not previously observed. If of himself, they have to do with certain poems he seems to be reading for the first time; or reading with a sense of power in them that startles him, for there had been no sign of it before. No poet has so changeable a surface as Hardy, no poet maintains in his reader so changeable a mind. Which are his best poems, and which are his worst? The question never seems to get settled; no wonder that he becomes the anthologist's despair.

Hardy himself has been before us in the cavern, lighting candles that would seem to show the way. Only, they do not show it all. They show, in fact, only their own wicks and tallow. They are the "philosophical" poems in which Hardy states his theory of life. It is the same theory that he states in *The Dynasts*, and it is equally unilluminating of anything save his own conscious thought. They are good poems, but they are not the ones that move us to call him a great poet. We want more from a poet than a theory of life; we want, if such a thing is possible, the look, feel, sound, taste, and even smell of life itself. And that is what Hardy eventually provides, and provides so richly that his name is sure to last. Meanwhile there are these philosophical poems which tell us that he finds no intelligibility in events, no form or order in the world. They are such poems as only he could write; they say what they have to say in his own idiom, for he meant very personally what he said in them; and they make a solemn, piercing music which alone would certify their sincerity. But they are not the heart of the book as he must have supposed they would be. They take their place among the thinner tissues, the ones with the least blood in them. The heart of the book, assuming it can be located at all, is older and tougher than these poems are. The book was not a single effort like *The Dynasts*, conceived and carried through with little or no interruption; it was the work of almost seventy years, and Hardy himself changed much in all that time. Or if he did not change, he submitted himself to many chances, and caught on the fly a bewildering number of perceptions which in the nature of things could not have been alike. An assiduous taker of notes upon himself, he rendered on a wide front his experience of the world, so that there is scarcely anything he has not understood and said before he is finished. This is not precisely to say that the rest of the book contradicts or denies the philosophical poems. Rather, it absorbs them; it finds a place for them and leaves them there.

In that place they say the same thing over and over: nature and man have come to a misunderstanding, and this misunderstanding will never be cured. Nature—sometimes the term is God—did not make man to think and feel; man was once unconscious, as other things still are, as mildews and mandrakes are, as stones and birds. That was the good time, when suffering of course existed yet could not tell itself it did; when no creature expected more than it could get; when the "disease of feeling" and the malady of thought had not yet been born in the brain of one creature, man, who now is doomed to pain by the very fact of this monstrous birth. The qualities we think distinguish us are the qualities that make us miserable. We long for what we can never have, just as we agonize over losses and failures of which nature takes only routine account. If we could be one with nature again, as Lucretius thought we could, and as naturalism says we must, we might recover that happiness of which we were unconscious when we had it; but this can never be. The gulf between us and our maker widens with every idea we have, and with every refinement of experience. Nature remains the same; we change, and in the process move away from her into a loneliness for which there is no remedy. The more we use our minds, the less we understand; yet we must keep on using our minds, as we must keep on hoping and despairing. Even nature is aware of all this, and laments her wayward child; though the only thing she can tell us is that if we came back to her we would be coming back to unconsciousness, we would be as toads and stars, as mushrooms and meteors.

> Maybe now
> Normal unawareness waits rebirth.

So in his last book, *Winter Words*, Hardy dares to hope; but it is the dimmest hope, and of the dimmest thing.

No wonder Hardy calls himself a tragic poet, and says on one occasion: "Comedy lies." No wonder he is at home with gloom, which he certainly is; or that he can note as a scientist would some signs that the world, like any other machine, is running down. In an uncanny poem, "Nature's Questioning," he even endows inanimate objects with the power to wonder what men wonder:

> When I look forth at dawning, pool,
> Field, flock, and lonely tree,
> All seem to gaze at me
> Like chastened children sitting silent in a school;
>
> Their faces dulled, constrained, and worn,
> As though the master's ways
> Through the long teaching days
> Had cowed them till their early zest was overborne.
>
> Upon them stirs in lippings mere
> (As if once clear in call,

But now scarce breathed at all)—
"We wonder, ever wonder, why we find us here!

"Has some Vast Imbecility,
Mighty to build and blend,
But impotent to tend,
Framed us in jest, and left us now to hazardry?

"Or come we of an Automaton
Unconscious of our pains? . . .
Or are we live remains
Of Godhead dying downwards, brain and eye now gone?"

These are terrible questions, put with a terrible candor, which of course is Hardy's. There is one further question, more difficult for Hardy to phrase because it seems to him rhetorical:

"Or is it that some high Plan betides,
As yet not understood,
Of Evil stormed by Good,
We the Forlorn Hope over which Achievement strides?"

He phrases it rather stuffily; he is not convinced that it was worth asking; but then he closes with music—his music— on the note most native to him:

Thus things around. No answerer I . . .
Meanwhile the winds, and rains,
And Earth's old glooms and pains
Are still the same, and Life and Death are neighbors nigh.

"Are still the same." Perhaps the heart of Hardy is just there. Winds and rains, and glooms and pains—those are the matter out of which he makes his art; they are the very folklore of his life, the familiar data, never to disappear, over which his imagination can pore without becoming tired. He would not know what to do without them; and once he said as much, in the poem he wrote refusing an invitation to the United States. Our claim to be young and happy was precisely what kept him away:

I shrink to seek a modern coast
Whose riper times have yet to be;

Where the new regions claim them free
From that long drip of human tears
Which peoples old in tragedy
Have left upon the centuried years.

No, he must remain where men, bent under pressures unimaginable in a new world, were all but deformed by pain and failure. His allegiance was to irony: to the monstrous coincidence, the ghastly event, or else—reducing calamity's scale—to the queer outcome, the miniature misadventure, the misery no bigger than a mouse. It was characteristic of Hardy that his poem about the sinking of the *Titanic* dealt with only one fact: the building of the iceberg and the building of the ship at whatever moment in each case would bring it about that the two collided when and where they did. But it was just as characteristic of him that he should write, in "The Sun on the Letter," about the odd circumstance that sunlight played as brightly over bad news as it would have over good. The size of things did not matter to him so long as all of them, huge or minute, testified to the principle of chance—or, as he put it in an early poem, Hap. Crass Casualty was still another name for it. And in nature as men once knew her it would not have been noticed, since nothing would have been noticed. It is the disease of feeling that has made men hypersensitive to truth: they cannot take what must be and what is. They are skinless creatures, shivering in the winds of circumstance.

Now it might follow from the firmness with which Hardy held on to this view that he would have no sympathy with those who feel; that he would spend all of his strength, as Lucretius did, in lecturing them upon the absurdity of their error; that he would, in other words, be cold and heartless. The contrary, as any reader of him knows, is true. In all the world there is no more feeling poet. He proves it in a hundred ways, no one of which is logically defensible; has he not demonstrated, even to monotony, the foolishness of tears? It is now that the great poet emerges, the poet whose humanity is profounder than his thought. He is that most moving kind of man, the kind that tries not to feel yet does; he is that most convincing of lovers, the one who begins by thinking he does not believe in love.

Hardy should scorn the emotions of himself and others; instead of which, he lets them break his heart.

The intensity of his concern may show itself in bizarre, unlikely ways, but there is no mistaking the intensity, as for example in "The Head Above the Fog," which gives life to a mistress in the very act of decapitating her:

> Something do I see
> Above the fog that sheets the mead,
> A figure like to life indeed,
> Moving along with spectre-speed,
> Seen by none but me.
>
> O the vision keen!—
> Tripping along to me for love
> As in the flesh it used to move,
> Only its hat and plume above
> The evening fog-fleece seen.
>
> In the day-fall wan,
> When nighted birds break off their song,
> Mere ghostly head it skims along,
> Just as it did when warm and strong,
> Body seeming gone.
>
> Such it is I see
> Above the fog that sheets the mead—
> Yea, that which once could breathe and plead!—
> Skimming along with spectre-speed
> To a last tryst with me.

The intensity in this case is not Hardy's, it is the ghost's, and the skimming speed of the ghost is what conveys it to us. Hardy is never without the power, indispensable in any ambitious poet, to endow his creations with an energy that seems to be their own. It is he who speaks, but it is they who have the final word. "The Head Above the Fog" treats of a tryst: a favorite subject with Hardy, for nothing interests him more than meetings between lovers; the most moving number for him is two. The meetings are more often sad than successful, but no matter; his deepest sympathies are engaged, and there is always something beautiful in that depth. He may or may not be recording a personal experience; most of the time, he tells us in his prefaces, he is not. It is clear enough that twenty-one poems in *Satires of Circumstance* have to do with the death of his first wife, with whom he had lived thirty-eight years; and these poems are seldom matched in all the literature of grief. Usually, however, we are willing to assume that he is dramatic, or as he himself liked to say, "personative." Whether or not the rule applies to the poem *Near Lanivet, 1872,* we could no more take it for unreal than we could so take *Othello* or *King Lear.*

There was a stunted handpost just on the crest,
Only a few feet high:
She was tired, and we stopped in the twilight-time for her rest,
At the crossroads close thereby.

She leant back, being so weary, against its stem,
And laid her arms on its own,
Each open palm stretched out to each end of them,
Her sad face sideways thrown.

Her white-clothed form at this dim-lit cease of day
Made her look as one crucified
In my gaze at her from the midst of the dusty way,
And hurriedly "Don't," I cried.

I do not think she heard. Loosing thence she said,
As she stepped forth ready to go,
"I am rested now.–Something strange came into my head;
I wish I had not leant so!"

And wordless we moved onward down from the hill
In the west cloud's murked obscure,
And looking back we could see the handpost still
In the solitude of the moor.

"It struck her too," I thought, for as if afraid
She heavily breathed as we trailed;
Till she said, "I did not think how 'twould look in the shade,
When I leant there like one nailed."

I, lightly: "There's nothing in it. For *you*, anyhow!"
–"O I know there is not," said she . . .
"Yet I wonder. . . . If no one is bodily crucified now,
In spirit one may be!"

And we dragged on and on, while we seemed to see
  In the running of Time's far glass
Her crucified, as she had wondered if she might be
  Some day.—Alas, alas!

His lovers are sometimes faithful, sometimes faithless; though as often as not the faithless ones are merely feeble of purpose, perhaps for a reason they cannot understand—they change, and are bewildered by the change. If they are cruel, it may be unintentionally so, or else they remain unaware that they were cruel. "A Maiden's Pledge" is the song of an absolutely faithful girl who will continue so even if her lover never hints of marriage:

Your comet-comings I will wait
With patience time shall not wear through.

Hardy takes pleasure in that, as in one of his best-known songs, "Let Me Enjoy," he says he takes pleasure in countless sweet things that are not for him.

Let me enjoy the earth no less
Because the all-enacting Might
That fashioned forth its loveliness
Had other aims than my delight. . . .

From manuscripts of moving song
Inspired by scenes and dreams unknown,
I'll pour out raptures that belong
To others, as they were my own.

His singular devotion to birds—one could almost say, his obsession with them—has something like this for its source. The intensity of birds, equal to his own, caught him up in their ecstasies as they sang or sported; or suffered, for he had no defenses against the spectacle of one in pain, particularly such a one as he addresses in "The Blinded Bird." His rage against men who run red-hot needles through the eyes of songbirds to increase the sweetness of their voices is stated only by indirection, yet the rage is strong enough:

Who hath charity? This bird.
Who suffereth long and is kind,

Is not provoked, though blind
And alive ensepulchred?
Who hopeth, endureth all things?
Who thinketh no evil, but sings?
Who is divine? This bird.

For Hardy, it would seem, birds were omens: they had been sent to tell him something. In "The Darkling Thrush" the message is that hope may have some meaning after all, for this bird if not for him. But another thrush, seen out of his window on Christmas day, told him something else again:

There, to reach a rotting berry,
Toils a thrush,—constrained to very
Dregs of food by sharp distress,
Taking such with thankfulness.

Why, O starving bird, when I
One day's joy would justify,
And put misery out of view,
Did you make me notice you?

Hardy never ceases to take testimony, to read the world as if it were a book, now closed, now open, with too many pages in it ever to let him finish. A tree in London can strike pity out of him because it is not in the country where it belongs. But sometimes it is he who is being read, as in the case of the fallow deer that looked in upon him one night:

We do not discern those eyes
  Watching in the snow;
Lit by lamps of rosy dyes
We do not discern those eyes
  Wondering, aglow,
  Fourfooted, tiptoe.

A poet's power to feel is best proved in the stories he tells, provided he can tell stories. Hardy could; that was where his genius lay; and so it may be that the heart of the *Collected Poems* beats in the narratives that throng it like so many persons, each one of them powerful in his or her own right. The final richness, perhaps, is here. Hardy is the envy of those who would be infinitely fertile in narrative ideas if only they could; it would seem to have been easy for him to be just that. Doubtless he worked harder than appears; there is evidence that he scoured newspapers for material, and took copious notes on stories he overheard in his native Wessex. The appearance, nevertheless, is of a fountain that cannot stop flowing; and its waters are strong waters that thrust forth from deep places. Hardy's stories are little melodramas, sensational, unrelenting, and if need be mournful beyond bearing, as the great ballads are.

In "The Burghers" a man who has planned to ambush his wife and her lover—to kill them with two strokes of his sword as they flee from his house—brings them home with him instead and heaps gifts upon them, of clothes and jewels; then he lets them go, knowing that his kindness to them is a wound which will never heal.

In "Her Death and After" a dying wife tells her former lover that she wishes the child she has just borne were his; her husband is not kind to her, and she fears for the child's future, since it is lame. The lover haunts her tomb until it becomes noticeable that he does; the husband himself notices it, and comes to ask him why; then without premeditation he tells the husband that the lame child is his. The child is sent to him and he brings it up, happily because this is what the dead woman would have wished, unhappily because he has hurt her name.

In "The Dance at the Phoenix" a woman of sixty who in her youth had been free with her favors, especially to "sundry troopers of the King's Own Cavalry," is now the virtuous wife of a gentle fellow who knows nothing of this past; and she would have died peacefully in good time had not on a certain evening the King's Cavalry come to the Phoenix Inn for a dance like those of the old days. Jenny, sleeping by her husband, hears the music and cannot refrain from slipping away to join the merriment, old as she is. She dances all night; is escorted home; slips back into bed; and dies of exhaustion which her husband attributes to some natural cause—"The King's said not a word."

In "A Sunday Morning Tragedy" a mother tells how, having failed to persuade her daughter's lover that he should marry her because she is with child by him, she procures from an herb woman a drug that will dispose of the child; only after she has administered the drug does she hear that the lover, repenting, has published the banns in church; but it is too late, for the drug proves fatal to the daughter.

In "The Noble Lady's Tale" the lady's husband, an actor who has given up the stage to please her father, begs her for permission to go back and play for just one night; she consents; he goes; but when he is home again he accuses her of having followed him to the theater, nor does he believe her oaths to the contrary; he finally decides that her wraith had followed him rather than herself in flesh and blood; but this distresses him quite as much, since it suggests that she had not trusted him; he wastes away, and so does she, unable to be sure whether a projection of her had pursued him; yet those who listen to her tale are left with further questions:

> Did she, we wonder, follow
>   Jealously?
> And were those protests hollow?—
>   Or saw he
> Some semblant dame? Or can wraiths really be?

In "The Moth-Signal" a woman, sitting with her husband one night, tells him she pities a moth that is burning in the candle flame; she goes outdoors to see how the weather is, and her lover comes to her from a tumulus nearby; he remarks that the moth she put out of the window as a lure to him is "burnt and broken," as he is, for he has shattered his own marriage vows; and an ancient Briton speaks from the tumulus, saying people are what they used to be.

In "The Sacrilege" a woman of the roads promises her lover that she will go no more to meet his rival, Wrestler Joe, provided he will steal treasure from the cathedral shrine with which she can buy ear-drops and rings; the lover sets off to do this, but only after engaging his brother to murder her in the event that the theft is traced to him (whereupon he will be hanged) and she then takes up with Wrestler Joe; things do go that way, and the brother drowns the woman, whose screams as she dies he will never cease to hear.

In a companion story, "A Trampwoman's Tragedy," the heroine pretends, for no reason she can understand in the sequel, that the child she carries is the child not of her "fancy-man" but of "Jeering John," his rival. Her fancy-man stabs Jeering John to death; is hanged; and leaves the woman wondering why she had done such a mad thing; her only comfort being that she can reassure the ghost of her lover whenever it appears and pleads to be told the truth.

In "The Statue of Liberty" a man is asked why he scrubs with mop and water the statue that stands in a city square; his answer is not that he is paid by the city guardians to do it, or that he loves liberty, which the statue symbolizes; it is simply that his daughter was the sculptor's model, and that she had died in this city, distant from his, before he could visit her; what he does now is the only favor he can do his darling, whose good name he thus preserves; but he does not know that he is speaking to the sculptor himself, and that the sculptor knows what happened to the daughter–she died "in the dens of vice."

And so on. The list seems to be endless, for Hardy's narrative vein does not run out. Now and then there is a hearty, humorous tale, since Hardy had that in him too: "The Bride-Night Fire," or "The Homecoming," the latter with a fine refrain:

> Gruffly growled the wind on Toller downland broad and bare,
> And lonesome was the house, and dark; and few came there.

But the prevailing tone is somber, and the accidents of love or hate, of innocence or guilt, are lighted by an artist in the wings who knows everything about shades and shadows.

He knows everything about time as well. Not only do his stories happen, as all stories do, in time; time is also his very subject. No poet has known better how to move forward and backward in this strangest of dimensions. The poem "One We Knew" concerns an old woman whose memories were pictures for others to study as well as herself:

She said she had often heard the gibbet creaking
  As it swayed in the lightning flash,
Had caught from the neighboring town a small child's shrieking
  At the cart-tail under the lash. . . .

With cap-framed face and long gaze into the embers—
  We seated around her knees—
She would dwell on such dead themes, not as one who remembers,
  But as one who sees.

She resembled Hardy in that, for his own memories were like things printed on a wall; anything that had happened to him, or had happened to his imagination, was real as present things were unable to be.

He lived in his own gallery of paintings; nor could he be sure how many of the figures there were ghosts. This philosopher who prided himself upon his hardness of mind saw ghosts; he had no business to, but he did. They were the spirits of murdered persons, or of persons otherwise wronged; but then too they could be of the mildest sort, like those in "The Garden Seat":

> At night when reddest flowers are black
> Those who once sat thereon come back;
> Quite a row of them sitting there,
> Quite a row of them sitting there.
>
> With them the seat does not break down,
> Nor winter freeze them, nor floods drown,
> For they are light as upper air,
> They are as light as upper air!

Perhaps the most touching of them all is to be found in the tale of the dead sailor's mother who comes nightly to the house where she used to live and waits for her son to appear; it is the only house he remembers, and so is the only one he can haunt.

Old houses interest anybody, but for Hardy they were tombs in which time was buried. But buried as it were alive, so that it moved there, and even spoke or sang there, like one of his authentic ghosts. An old mirror, he assumed, must be haunted by the images that had been made upon it; one of his poems, "The Cheval-Glass," tells of a man who bought at an auction the mirror before which a woman he once had loved stood nightly and brushed her hair; he said he saw her in it still, and would keep it with him till he died. Old furniture must remember, Hardy thought, the people who had used it; indeed it must reflect them:

> Hands upon hands, growing paler and paler,
> As in a mirror a candle-flame
> Shows images of itself, each frailer
> As it recedes, though the eye may frame
> Its shape the same.

There was not too much difference for Hardy between an old English house and a prehistoric tumulus or barrow, or a Roman ruin: those had been houses too, if only for bones. The bones still slept there; they even dreamed, and he could hear them talking in their sleep. But the official antiquities of his island were really no older for him than things he himself had seen or done long years ago. Time, that relative thing, was so relative in his case that a certain Roman road on which as a child he had walked with his mother was ancient to him rather for this reason than for the reason that helmed legionaries once marched along it. His imagination had always a temporal cast. His genius could endow things with age that had none otherwise, just as it could read into a single moment, recollected and reconsidered, eternities of meaning which as it passed had not been recognized; the present moment, he is forever saying, contains all time and more, but nobody knows this then. Railway trains and stations, despite their bleakness, which he never minimizes, take on in his poems the dignity of timeless crossroads where anything on earth can happen, or anything in hell or heaven.

His love of music is chiefly the love of country singing—old singing, of songs and hymns not much remembered now. His poems ring with the quaint names of former tunes, just as they shake with the feet of dancers: not merely her of the Phoenix Inn, but countless young and old performers of forgotten steps. Church choirs, and groups of warblers by night, serenading bridegrooms or celebrating births and deaths—these have a peculiar, almost a sacred importance for Hardy, who knows the names of ancient instruments, too, and is learned in the folklore of bells. One of his best stories, "The Chapel-Organist," deals with a woman who would rather die than cease to play

> Old Hundredth, Saint Stephen's,
> Mount Zion, New Sabbath, Miles-Lane, Holy Rest, and Arabia, and Eaton.

And the whole subject comes perfectly into focus as he watches some young girls in a winter street singing songs whose origins are venerable beyond their comprehension:

> Yea, old notes like those
> Here are living on yet!—
> But of their fame and fashion
> How little these know
> Who strum without passion
> For pence in the snow!

Hardy hugged time to himself as he hugged pain and gloom; they were the three dimensions of his universe, in which he felt so much at home that he could be surprised when readers complained of its barrenness. It was thick and warm for him, like an old coat that exactly fitted him, even if it looked a little long, and indeed drooped to the ground. It was what he recognized as reality, the one thing to which he was entirely committed. The bitterness of the world did not forbid him to embrace it: a poor thing, but his own. At times, to be sure, he wondered whether he missed something that others saw; he peered hard, and had the reward of any pessimist—something was better than he expected. For that matter, many things were; even all things, if one did not mind their being just what they were. Now and then he would offer an apology for the low tones in which he spoke: he but sang his part, as others must sing theirs. There is in fact much kindness in him, a sort of subdued good nature which shines through his frown as well as his smile; for he smiled and was humorous, too, he had a nice sense of the absurd. He was susceptible to superstitions for which his philosophy would have had no use. Oxen *might* kneel on Christmas Eve; and of course there were all those ghosts; there was true love, too, a thing that mechanism would not explain.

His mind was complicated, and so was his art. The effect of plainness in his poems can make us overlook their skill: a conscious thing with him, and the product of study. He seems to be interested in nothing but accuracy of statement, even if this means that he must sometimes sound clumsy and crude; exactness is what he wants, and he will sacrifice everything to it. This is true; and it is true of any great poet; there is nothing else that causes us in the end to love poetry at all. But accuracy is itself an art, a fine and high one which all the muses conspire to praise. Hardy's muses, he said in 1887, were five in number: Form, Tune, Story, Dance, and Hymn. The last of these may surprise us a little until we read him through again and realize how often he was lyric in the rich, free, leaping way of the Elizabethans:

> This is the weather the cuckoo likes,
>   And so do I;
> When showers betumble the chestnut spikes,
>   And nestlings fly:
> And the little brown nightingale bills his best,
> And they sit outside at "The Travellers' Rest,"
> And maids come forth sprig-muslin drest,
> And citizens dream of the south and west,
>   And so do I.

Or until we remember how various his stanzas are; he studied the stanza like a musician, and made it his idiom, whether intricate as in "The Discovery":

> I wandered to a crude coast
>     Like a ghost;
> Upon the hills I saw fires–
>     Funeral pyres
> Seemingly–and heard breaking
> Waves like distant cannonades that set the land shaking;

or simple as in "The Pine Planters (Marty South's Reverie)":

We work here together
  In blast and breeze;
He fills the earth in,
  I hold the trees.

He does not notice
  That what I do
Keeps me from moving
  And chills me through . . .

I have helped him so many,
  So many days,
But never win any
  Small word of praise!

Hardy was a musician; he was also an etcher. It was not for nothing that he had practiced architecture; the draftsman in him is always coming out. He has the keen eye that feeling cannot confuse—an old man's eye, we are tempted to say, which misses nothing. Some of his poems are pure studies in black and white of things he saw in passing: "An East-End Curate," for example, or "No Buyers: A Street Scene," or "Nobody Comes." Others are masterpieces with weather for their theme: any kind of weather, for Hardy liked it all, but his specialty was rain, as in "A Sheep Fair":

The day arrives of the autumn fair,
  And torrents fall,
Though sheep in throngs are gathered there,
  Ten thousand all,
Sodden, with hurdles round them reared:
And, lot by lot, the pens are cleared,
And the auctioneer wrings out his beard,
And wipes his book, bedrenched and smeared,
And rakes the rain from his face with the edge of his hand,
  As torrents fall.

The wool of the ewes is like a sponge
  With the daylong rain:
Jammed tight, to turn, or lie, or lunge,
  They strive in vain.
Their horns are soft as finger-nails,

Their shepherds reek against the rails,
The tied dogs soak with tucked-in tails,
The buyers' hat-brims fill like pails,
Which spill small cascades when they shift their stand
In the daylong rain.

Not that these particular sheep were before him as he wrote; a third stanza of the poem says it was long ago that he went to Pummery Fair, "and the hoarse auctioneer is dead." But time had not faded the impression—time, the sixth muse of Thomas Hardy.

The world of the *Collected Poems* is a great world. It is *the* great world, seen always as Hardy saw it, with quizzical, deep eyes that both formed and deformed it. But the deformation was no crime; it was rather a style, a way of twisting things into the shape his genius saw. This is often a queer shape. What other poet, wishing to tell his beloved that he would be hers even in the grave, ever expressed the hope

That thy worm should be my worm, Love?

Worms were as much his specialty as weather.

The leaf drops: earthworms draw it in
At night-time noiselessly.

That is a small event among the many that take place in the great world. But Hardy noticed it, and having noticed it he must put it down. Of the several epitaphs he composed for himself, none is more simple and true than "Afterwards," with this refrain to be spoken by his neighbors:

"He was a man who used to notice such things."

# Joseph and His Brothers: A Comedy in Four Parts

*(To Maurice Samuel)*

TO SAY that Mann's *Joseph and His Brothers* is primarily a comic work is to say no more than the author himself said in his foreword to the new edition of 1948. He called it then "a humorous song of mankind," an "epic undertaking" in the spirit of Goethe rather than of Wagner, a narrative written "playfully," with many "pleasantries" in it which he hoped would "cheer those who come after us," though with "pathos" in it too which at some later time might still be touching. He spoke of it, that is to say, as a comic poem of vast proportions. And so it is. Its "seventy thousand calmly flowing lines"—someone else might say its twelve hundred continuously intelligent pages—make up a modern masterpiece with which there are few things to be compared, though Marcel Proust's *Remembrance of Things Past* is surely one of those. That equally vast work depends equally with *Joseph and His Brothers* upon our sense of time; or, if you prefer, upon our sense of eternity; or, if you insist, upon our sense of the present moment. For when we have succeeded in giving ourselves to the present moment we are as near to eternity as we shall ever get. Eternity is not a lot of time; it is no time at all, and so is this moment that passes before we know it has come—except that we do know some moments when they come, and it is these and only these from which we learn.

The comic genius loves to speculate about such matters. It has not always done so as explicitly as in the two outstanding cases of Proust and Mann; but then ours is an explicit age which struggles to be conscious of everything, so that we are not surprised when Mann discusses at length a number of things that Chaucer, say, could take for granted. The comic genius has never been more alive than it was in Chaucer, but it does not appear that he thought he needed a theory of time, or at any rate a statable one which in effect would constitute his subject matter. Neither of course does Mann think simply that; his subject matter after all is never anything but Joseph and his father and his brothers, and the wonderful world of Egypt where he spent his most brilliant years, just as in *The Magic Mountain*, Mann's other masterpiece which deals with time, the subject matter is whatever the persons of the story talk about when their excellent brains catch fire in the cold solitude of an Alpine sanatorium. Yet it is true that Mann must think out loud as he writes, and what he thinks about is the bottomless well of time which threatens, if looked into deeply enough, to obscure every individual character and countenance —even those of Joseph himself—and to silence every event so that we who come long after may have doubts that it occurred, or in any case that it made much noise in the universe it could not manage at the end to alter. The famous prelude to the work, called Descent into Hell, might have been called instead Descent into Time. The genius of story can never dispense with time, but the genius of comic story stands in a peculiar relation to that commodity. It both believes in it and does not. Tragedy believes furiously, even obsessively, in time; time always presses there, leaving the hero unfree to act in the wise way he might if he had the leisure. Comedy, on the other hand, relaxes and disperses time; spreads it out or draws it thin so that it looks a little like eternity. It is not eternity, and cannot ever be; but enough of it will establish the perspective that comedy likes and indeed must have. Only, given the maximum perspective, movement comes to a stop and men are reduced to resembling one another so closely, even so absurdly, that merely man is left; or, to put it abstractly, human nature.

Perhaps it was human nature that Mann lived with during the sixteen dreadful years, between 1926 and 1942, when he was composing *Joseph and His Brothers.* One could also say that he lived with Joseph, the individual upon whose image he had settled. But the image enlarged while he studied it, as did the image of every other person in the tale, so that at last he had before him something like the whole spectacle which human life provides when nothing operates to distort it. In the Germany of these years it was outrageously distorted, and there were those who said it would never regain its ancient shape. Here, though, was that very shape; and Mann has testified to the satisfaction he derived from contemplating its breadth and depth. "It was my refuge, my comfort, my home," he says, "my symbol of steadfastness, the guarantee of my perseverance in the tempestuous change of things."

Yet he would have done substantially as he did in any case. Mann's genius was entirely comic; which is to say that it was contemplative, discursive, skeptical, tender, mocking, and loving all at once. It was contemplative because it desired the oldest and the widest view of things, somewhat as they are, supposing man can know this, in their eternal aspect. It was discursive because man's mind is most at home in conversation, in endless talk that considers, measures, analogizes, and compares. No reader of Mann needs to be told how irresistibly he was drawn to language, and how much pleasure he took in imitating the various dialects of thought. The comic genius is among other things a mimic; so in America, where Mann wrote the fourth section of his epic, it was natural for him not merely to see a parallel between Joseph the Provider and Roosevelt the prophet of abundance, but also to adopt so many idioms of the time and place as to incur the charge that he no longer wrote in German, though of course he did, to the enrichment of that none too lively language.

*The Magic Mountain,* like any pure comedy, tends to be all conversation; and if this is not quite true of the Joseph books, it is nevertheless true that what its people say to one another, and what Mann says about them as he converses with his reader, can be understood as carrying most of the burden. Nor can one miss the fact that Joseph's own gift, his distinguishing art, is the wonderful way he has with words, so that he entrances all who come within the sound of his voice or—the same thing—the reach of his mind. When he read aloud to Potiphar it was as if he were creating a new beauty in the text. The intellect of any person is perhaps most swiftly revealed by the way he reads a page he has never seen before. Potiphar knew the pages by heart, but never had they sounded like this. "Joseph read . . . capitally," we hear; "was fluent, exact, unaffected, moderately dramatic, with such natural command of words that the most involved literary style had a happy conversational ease. Literally he read himself into the heart of the listener; and when we seek to understand his swift rise in the Egyptian's favor we must by no means leave out of account these reading hours." He knew his way among intricate phrases as Hamlet, speaking to the players, knew his; no mind, no tongue, has ever been more nimble than that. But this was Hamlet in his comic aspect: his original aspect, which tragedy, as Ophelia divines, has already overwhelmed and lamentably deformed.

The genius of Mann is skeptical in the finest sense of an often misapprehended term. It was not that he believed nothing; he believed everything; he liked ideas, and could live with all of them at once. No sooner did one start up in his brain than another came to reinforce, illuminate, or check it. This was why he could turn so soon from tenderness to pathos, and why he could mock the very man he loved the most. These transformations of his mood will bewilder anyone who does not comprehend how serious at last the comic spirit is. Nothing in man is more serious than his sense of humor; it is the sign that he wants all the truth, and sees more sides of it than can be soberly and systematically stated; it is the sign, furthermore, that he can remember one idea even while he entertains another, and that he can live with contradiction. It is the reason at any rate that we cannot take seriously one whose mind and heart have never been known to smile. The gods do not weep; they smile. Eternity is something like the sun.

The comic spirit has a perfect sense of time, as of a good

comedian we say that he has perfect timing. The comic spirit knows that time both does and does not exist; it can look like sheer illusion, though the illusion is one in which comedy will luxuriously live. Comedy takes its time, as truth and history do. The good story-teller is never in a hurry, nor do we want him to be; his digressions, his elaborations, his hesitations, his gestures are in the end more interesting than the action he unfolds; we do not, in fact, want him to reach the end, for then we shall no longer hear his voice or relish with him the way he looks at life, of which the story at hand is but one illustration. While it was being told it amply sufficed our hunger for understanding; it replaced all other stories; was, in effect, story itself, was poetry in the flesh. It treated of only a few people and things, and it treated them in some present moment which absorbed us so that we forgot the rest of time. Yet it had also something to do with the rest of time, which hung about it like a haze, beautifying and validating its apparently random, its artfully accidental details. "The form of timelessness," says Mann, "is the here and now." He can say this because he knows how to see Joseph and Jacob as men who lived both long ago and now. They lived so long ago that if time were altogether and simply real they would have no identity today; their figures, their faces, would be woefully indistinct, and the thoughts they had would be mere puffs of desert dust. But time is not that real; Joseph and Jacob can exist not only again but yet; because they existed so intensely in their moment they live always, in all moments. These things are forever happening. History, with a monotony which comedy loves rather than deplores, repeats itself ad infinitum. All thoughts, all things, all men are simultaneously true, as somehow in God's mind they are. The mind of comedy is not that great, but it is the greatest possession of the one creature made in God's image—unless, as Mann playfully suggests, man was the maker of God: in the person of Abram was none other than His father. But in that case it would still be true that the greatest thing in man is his power to know and remember many things at once; to master time; to be in a word the receptacle of the comic spirit.

Any story that is worth telling can be told either briefly or at length. Ideally these alternatives are absolute: the teller takes no time at all, or else he takes an infinite amount of it. Since neither of those miracles is possible, the narrative artist must be content with a choice between abridgement and amplitude. Mann certainly did not abridge the story of Joseph. His work is forty-five times as long as the section of *Genesis* which deals with the hero alone, and fifteen times as long as the section which covers in addition, as Mann himself does, the careers of Abraham, Isaac, and Jacob. This is amplitude indeed, and there have been those who wondered whether Mann did not achieve too much of it for any earthly purpose. The answer ought to be clear. His purpose was comic, and comedy takes its time. It insists upon leisure, of which it is confident that there cannot be too much. Also it is addicted to talk, its own and others', and entertains itself with as much of that as the subject suggests, or as we shall listen to. The subject of Joseph suggested everything to Mann; nothing he knew or thought was alien to it, and no idea was irrelevant. So for sixteen years, with major and minor interruptions, he happily spun his web until it draped like a silken veil the whole figure of the world.

Even *Genesis* had lingered over the story as it did not in the cases of Abraham, Isaac, and Jacob. There was something special about Joseph even then and there; he had nothing of the patriarch about him, and in after times his name dropped out of the Bible. God appeared to Moses as the God of three great men, not four. Joseph had saved the race in Egypt, but he was never to be honored as one of its founders. He was not simple enough for that. Neither in a sense was Jacob, yet Jacob's name lived on as one of the never-to-be-forgotten three. Jacob for one thing did not become an Egyptian; he never became anything but what he was, so that when Joseph met him in the Land of Goshen there was a fantastic difference between the two figures: the younger one brilliant with linen and gold, the older one as plain as the wagon seat on which he had ridden all the way from Israel, through dust and among the remnant of his herds. It was not easy for the father to recognize his son in the splendid prince he saw step out of a chariot; nor, when the time came to talk, did he hesitate to say some things that may have sounded bitter to the young man whose mind was full of the glittering deeds he knew he had done. "God has . . . given you back, but yet not quite, for He has kept you too. . . . He has elevated and rejected you both in one, I say it in your ear, beloved child, and you are wise enough to be able to hear it. He has raised you above your brothers just as in your dream—but He has raised you in a worldly way, not in the sense of salvation and the inheritance of the blessing. . . . You are blessed, my dear one, . . . blessed with blitheness and with destiny, with wit and with dreams. Still, it is a worldly blessing, not a spiritual one. . . . Through you salvation is not to reach the peoples and the leadership is denied you. . . . You are not like the fathers, my child, for you are no spiritual prince, but a worldly one." This is Mann writing, not the author of *Genesis*, but it is what the whole Bible means in spite of its silence on the subject. The Bible is silent like the patriarchs; Mann, like Joseph, is eloquent as civilization and comedy are eloquent. He is even loquacious, for there is nothing he would rather do than put into words what simple men suppose cannot be said, or for that matter has no need to be said.

There can be no comedy about patriarchs. They come before civilization is in flower, and comedy is the finest of the flowers. They are the foundation, for the most part hidden from sight; it is the cornice, the gables, and the roof. Or, to change the figure once again, they are the blood and it is the complexion. Mann's Joseph is all grace, all light, all intellect at its highest. He can do anything except be the silent, tremendous man each one of his ancestors was. In Egypt he remembers the faith of his fathers, and characteristically gives a lucid account of it whenever asked. But it is not a part of him; it is not in his bones as it is in the bones of Jacob. If anything he understands it too perfectly; it is one of the works of art he knows like a connoisseur; it is outside him, and he can leave it there when he likes. He leaves it there during his sundry flirtations with other faiths and other deities: Tammuz, Ashtaroth, and Osiris. What Mann calls "the soul's love-affair with matter" fascinates him if anything too much. There was a youthful moment when he almost worshiped the

Moon and subscribed to its cult. "As a cult," says Mann, "it was vague, confused, and prone to degenerate—calculated to alarm the careful father—but just on that ground intoxicating, because mental and physical emotions were therein so enchantingly mixed." Egypt, the Kingdom of the Dead and therefore the embodiment of all that Jacob had taught him to abhor, was not visited by Joseph voluntarily; Jacob's other sons, the red-eyed sons of Leah, sent him there; but once there he again became the connoisseur of customs, in this case exquisite ones which the artist in him could not but admire. He did no more than admire and master this new way of life; he remained faithful to his fathers, and said so often enough; yet none of his fathers could have done what he did—could have become more Egyptian than any son of Egypt, and worn its manners like so many jewels. It is impossible to imagine Isaac, for example, flattering as Joseph did the guide who was about to take him in to his first audience with Pharaoh. Isaac would never have been there in the first place; but supposing that he was, and supposing that the guide asked him whether he knew how to salute the god, it never could have occurred to him to smile and say: "I wish I did not, for it would be pleasant to learn it of you." This was flattery, and it was mockery too; it came from the top of Joseph's mind, that touched the stars.

Joseph is material for comedy precisely because he is civilized. Both comedy and tragedy depend on civilization for their power. The stories of the patriarchs belong perhaps in neither category; they are too primitive, possibly they are too important, to be classified at all. They simply exist and tell themselves, as seeds are sown in the ground. The first fathers were to be sure the heroes of great stories; they were this side of God in whose life there were no events; but they were nowhere near as far away from absolute simplicity as Joseph was. Joseph was secular; he could believe anything and everything; he was advanced; he was free; and his only illusion was that he had none. He had several concerning himself, the chief of these being that there was no real difference between him and Jacob. Even at the end he was not too certain as to what the difference was that Jacob had tried his best to put into words. This supremely intelligent man did not, that is to say, know everything. And just there is the point at which he becomes available for comic treatment. The stupid person who knows nothing is of no interest to the comic spirit. The brilliant person who nevertheless is blind to something as visible as the ground before his feet—he is the one upon whom wit delights to sharpen its knives. And so with Joseph in Mann's case. Loving his hero as he loved himself, Mann still could mock him because he was not God. And in the same breath he could adore him. He lavished upon him all the understanding that he had, all the elaboration of which his wit was so abundantly capable. Mann's marvelous reconstructions of the Egyptian court, intricate perhaps beyond any imagination but his, and ornate as only he could delicately achieve ornateness—witness for example the entrance of Nefertiti, "with swaying tread, faintly smiling, her eyes cast down, the long, lovely neck thrust anxiously out: the bearer of the seed of the sun"—still do not match the work he did inside Joseph's mind, where recess upon recess opens as it were into the very caverns of genius. And this work is endless; it fills a fearsome multitude of pages; nor was any of it done in *Genesis*. It is all Mann, all modern, and all comedy.

Sometimes, to be sure, Mann wonders to himself about his method, and lets us know that he does so. "There is too much abridgement and condensation about this," he suddenly remarks of the Biblical narrative where it puts in two sentences the decision of Pharaoh to set Joseph over all Egypt; "it is too dry, it is a drawn and salted and embalmed remnant of the truth, not truth's living lineaments." Within a few lines, however, he has remembered the contrary principle. "Of course," he continues, "there is really nothing against condensation in itself. In the long run it is quite impossible to narrate life just as it flows. What would it lead to? Into the infinite. It would be beyond human powers. Whoever got such an idea fixed in his head would not only never finish, he would be suffocated at the outset. Entangled in a web of desultory exactitude, a madness of detail. No, excision must play its part at the beautiful feast of narration and recreation; it has an important and indispensable role. Here, then, the art will be judiciously practised, to the end of getting finally quit of a preoccupation which, though after all it has a distant kinship with the attempt to drink the sea dry, must not be driven to the extreme and utter folly of actually and literally doing so."

Yet three hundred pages before this he had burst out in the same way, and in the same way had taken his words back. The question then was how Potiphar's wife had offered herself to Joseph. "To tell the truth," exclaimed Mann on that occasion, "I am horrified at the briefness and curtness of the original account, which does so little justice to life's bitter circumstantiality. Seldom have I felt more acutely the harm done to truth by abbreviation and compression. Yet let no one think that I am deaf to the reproach—whether expressed or, out of politeness, not expressed—which hangs over my account, my entire exposition: to the effect that the laconic terseness of the original text cannot be surpassed, and that my whole enterprise, which is already of such long continuance, is so much labor lost. But since when, may I ask, does a commentator set himself up in competition with his text? And besides, is there not as much dignity and importance attached to the discussion of the 'how' as to the transmission of the 'what'? Let us remind ourselves once again that before the story was first told, it had to tell itself—with an exactitude of which life alone is master, and to attain which a narrator has no hope or prospect at all. He can only approach it by serving the 'how' of life more faithfully than the lapidary spirit of the 'what' condescended to do. But if ever the fidelity of a commentator can justify itself, then surely it does in the story of Potiphar's wife and of just what, according to the tradition, she is supposed to have said."

Doubtless in such passages Mann protests too much, and in doing so loses his good humor. The comic spirit cannot afford to worry about its right to exist. And most of the time in Mann it does not commit that fault. Most of the time it is vigorous and blithe, and goes about its business with its head high in the air. Nor does it call that business commentary. It calls it story, and lets us add that it is comedy too.

Mann's method of amplification is simple in one sense: it is the method of filling in, of stuffing interstices with matter he thinks belongs there. The Biblical narrative is famously bald;

it leaves almost everything to the imagination, after of course giving the imagination great work to do. Mann cannot be said to desire that nothing be left for his own reader to imagine; he too gives him work, and it can be a life's work if one chooses to do it; but the reader in this case has ideas to contemplate rather than actions to complete. And the ideas are Mann's. Claiming to know in full detail what the people of the ancient tale said to one another in this crisis or that, he supplies conversations which themselves are food for thought, so delicate and deep are they. The colloquies between Jacob and his favorite son explore the entire field of filial and paternal feeling. What Pharaoh said to Joseph tells us more about Egypt than the archaeologists can. And what Potiphar's wife confessed to him in her third-year agony of love is the climax of a whole fine novel of which she has been the distinguished heroine—though in Mann's opinion Joseph has not been its distinguished hero. He gives us that opinion—it has to do with Joseph's vanity—just as he always lays bare for us the process of his own thought. We are continuously in his confidence; the book could in fact be described as a conversation between the author and the reader, or rather as a monologue which the reader is expected to overhear. To that extent it *is* a commentary.

But the method is not as simple as all that. Sometimes it involves the addition of circumstances and deeds, the outright invention of narrative details, none of which we could have worked out for ourselves unless our talent and our scholarship had been identical with Mann's. And the richest number of these is to be found in the Potiphar section, which Mann himself called "the artistic zenith of the work." Potiphar's household becomes a fascinating world all by itself. The dwarfs, the parents of the master, the eunuch master and his tragic wife—these are the central figures, and each one of them is a triumph of creation, yet they are surrounded by others still, in a busy and beautiful house which for the time being absorbs our entire attention. And none of this is in the Bible. Perhaps it did not need to be, but we do not think of that; and even if we did we would find nothing that contradicted or violated the primitive fable. It is simply that Mann has moved us up close enough for us to be able to see what happened in this household day by day—it may be minute by minute—during the three years it was a part of human history. There is the day, for instance, of the ladies' party, when Potiphar's wife, incapable any longer of bearing alone the crushing burden of her love for Joseph, invites her friends to come and eat oranges with her. Each of them is given a little, sharp knife with which to open the precious fruit; each starts to do so at the moment when Joseph appears to pour the wine; and down each snow-white wrist runs a stream of crimson blood. For so much beauty, so suddenly entering the hall, has captured each lady's eyes, so that her knife knows not where it should cut. And this was exactly as Mut had planned it when she told Joseph he must come in among them at such and such a moment. It is an unforgettable moment; nor did Mann need to invent it. His scholarship, which surely was enormous, found it for him in the Koran, in seventeen Persian poems, and in "countless renderings by pencil and brush." Those are the sources he reveals to us; but if we have access to none of them we can go to Louis Ginzberg's *Legends of the Jews* for a version graphic enough.

Not that Mann inserts the episode of the ladies' party with a flourish of narrative trumpets or with any brave show of art. Here also he is true to the comic tradition of story-telling, which plays down the narrative art. It says that history is more interesting than fiction; so history is what it pretends to write. Chaucer has his "author" whom he merely follows; Cervantes has his Arabian biographer whom he merely translates. The comic artist will not admit that he has invented anything; the truth is enough for him—Mann says "the facts"—and all truth is as old as the hills anyway; there can be no new stories, just as there can be nothing new under the sun; see the Bible as to that. Every man knows everything; except of course that some men forget what they know, or do not wholly realize it, and so commit the only sin that comedy is designed to deal with, namely folly. Folly is not a fatal sin, though there are those who unaccountably grow fond of it in themselves; therefore it either can be cured or can be rendered harmless as a spectacle at which we wiser ones may smile. It is rendered harmless by understanding: the fool's understanding at last, or if this is not to be expected, then ours; and probably, too, that of several other persons in the story.

The essence of comedy is its love of understanding. That is why it goes in so heavily for talk—or rather, we hope, lightly: deliciously and lightly. The dialectic of comedy may seem queer, but it is dialectic nevertheless; and they are right who credit Plato with having perfected both philosophy and comedy in his matchless dialogues. Now it would be saying too much, if not too little, to say that the essence of tragedy is misunderstanding. The errors of tragic heroes are too vast to be so trivially dismissed. Yet they do misunderstand their situations and themselves; and in the rush of events which their own blindness accelerates they do dreadful things which with more time and light they would never have done. Tragedies are dark and short; more light, more time, more talk would make literally all the difference in the world; but those blessings are not available. Whereas they are the very stuff of comedy, which like John Tanner keeps on talking though the heavens fall. But in fact they do not fall. In comedy there is neither the midnight of utter confusion nor the sudden blaze of a belated dawn. In comedy the hour is always noon.

And nothing much happens then. The action of any comedy is less interesting—certainly less memorable—than the discussions it contains. A tragedy whose plot cannot be remembered in the strict order of its events is no tragedy at all; the events must create their own order, from which there is no escape, or else they will have no meaning for the mind. This must have been what Aristotle meant when he said the soul of a tragedy was its plot; the action was everything. In comedy there is action too, or we should have no story; but it is most interesting for what can be said about it before and after it is done. Which throws still further light upon the fact that comic poets underplay their plots and take no responsibility for them in the first place. By the same token they are indifferent to dramatic or narrative effects; they ignore the conventional devices for securing such effects; they lean over backwards to avoid melodrama, which to be sure they may approach as a possibility, but which they would rather parody than embrace.

So Mann in his great comedy refuses to make what tragedy would make, and what the Bible did make, out of certain recognition scenes. The recognition scene is essential to tragedy, which lives on such bursts of feeling as it perfectly provides. There was an opportunity for Mann to contrive a meeting between Joseph and Mut-em-enet after Joseph came home from prison. But he discusses the possibility only to reject it. Romancers, he says, have tried their hands at such a scene, and the result is "Persian musk," is "attar of roses," which is to say sweet nonsense. For one thing "it has nothing to do with the facts." For another, their story was done.

Even the recognition scenes which he is bound to accept because they come down to him and are a part of his duty—those between Joseph and his brothers at the climax and between Jacob and Joseph at the very end—he deliberately muffs, and here and there mocks. Of course they are moving; but Mann does not want them to break our hearts, and he knows how to keep them from doing so. He wraps them in talk; the principals murmur to each other even while they weep; dialectic still holds the center of the stage. And as for the weeping, what would a tragic poet have to say of one who in the immortal scene between Joseph and his brothers transmogrifies the Biblical "he wept aloud" into: "His nose began to prickle inside, he sniffed a little, and his eyes all at once ran over?" Granted, on a later page—much later, for the scene is long—we are told that "glittering tears ran down his cheeks." This to be sure is more like drama; yet even there we are forced to suspect that the tears of Joseph *would* glitter, since everything about him shines.

Nor at the moment when the great scene was preparing had the author kept us in suspense as to whether it would happen. The comic artist cares nothing for suspense, which indeed is never as indispensable to narrative as commonly it is thought to be. It is at best a second-rate device for generating interest where no interest naturally exists. At least this is true if it consists of no more than the artificial withholding from us of some information we need for understanding and would normally have. When it consists of telling us that a given thing will happen but letting us wait to see how it happens, and precisely when, it is a powerful because a natural narrative tool. And it is thus that Mann uses it, and confides to us that he does. "Joseph's suspense was great," he writes on one occasion; "on this point depended his future relations with the brothers. We, of course, are in no suspense: we know all the phases of the story by heart. . . . So in our wisdom we may smile at him."

Such, remarks Mann on an earlier occasion, is the advantage of having an old story to retell. "If I were here a mere inventor of tales, what I have to tell would certainly expose me to the reproach of drawing too long a bow, and presuming far too much upon a credulity which after all has its limits. Luckily, such is not my role. I rest upon the traditional facts, which are not less sound because some of them ring as though they were newly minted. Thus I am in a position to state what I have to tell in an assured and tranquil tone that in the face of all doubts and reproaches carries conviction." A tragic poet who stopped his story to address his audience thus would instantly break his spell and lose all power to convince. For the comic poet there is no spell; or if there is one and its name is truth, it is just in this offhand way that he invokes it.

The truth about Joseph is of course a complicated thing which it is the main business of the book to convey. Mann's hero is perhaps not different from the one we meet in *Genesis*, nor is his father altered from the ancient Jacob; nor for that matter is their relation to each other built here upon ground which the original text did not at least lay out. But Mann's refinements are as many as they are marvelous. The brilliance and beauty of Joseph have few parallels in the fiction of the world. And the vanity. The problem was to make the vanity palatable, and it was solved by suggesting, not indeed in so many words, that it was like the vanity of a golden mirror which can no more help being what it is than a bright person can help being bright. Joseph might have bitten off his tongue, as Potiphar's poor wife all but did; yet he did not; he kept on saying with it the most fascinating and impudent things; and we are as glad of this as Jacob was, or Benjamin, or even the ten sullen half-brothers who in spite of themselves adored the speaker of them too at the same time that they wanted to kill him, or at least to remove him from their sight forever. It was Jacob, however, who resisted Joseph least; which is a mild way of saying that he committed the sin of idolatry by elevating him to the rank of favorite son, somewhat as he had committed the same sin by loving Rachel for herself and not in God. Mann is willing to say that the doting father was the chief source of his son's misery, if misery it was. Perhaps it was never that; for the pits into which this youth was cast, first in the desert and then in Egypt, yielded in every case an experience he could dramatize; and there was no exercise he loved more.

In no crisis of his life did Joseph die so that he might be reborn. He does not look to us at the end like one of those truly great men of whom it can be said not that they have lived a lot but that they have died a lot—have been, we sometimes say, in hell. No, in some amazing way he has not been touched by the bonfires he walked through. For one thing, though he would deny this, he has never ceased to assume that others must love him more than they love themselves. The assumption had been wrong both in the case of his brothers and in that of Mut-em-enet, and now he knows that it was wrong. Yet he has not changed in the secret depths of his heart where he still knows that he is like nobody else. "Have you ever heard the voice of self-denying love?" Jacob asks him this in the Land of Goshen, and the question answers itself. When on the last page of the book Joseph insists to his brothers that they are to forgive him, not he to forgive them, he speaks in the character he has enjoyed from the beginning. "If it is a question of pardon between us human beings, then it is I myself must beg for it, for you had perforce to be cast in the villain's part so that things might turn out as they did." The hero's part had been so naturally his that he still needs no rehearsing in it.

Not that we love him less because all this is true. The triumph of Mann is that we love on every page the hero he himself loves this side of idolatry. Idolatry in Mann would have destroyed his comedy, since comedy admits no gods that are made of earth. That he resisted the sin, tempted though he surely was, is a triumph more stupendous still. The sign of his resistance is the impression of Joseph he leaves with us at last:

the impression of one whose understanding is so fine that the light in his mind almost puts out the stars—yet not those stars at which his great-grandfather Abraham, that wonderful old man, stared without speaking a single word. "One can easily be in a story," Mann has Joseph say, "and not understand it." Joseph understood everything in his story except himself. His light never shone altogether inward, producing perfect silence.

# Don Quixote's Profession

*(To Frederick W. Dupee)*

I

A GENTLEMAN of fifty, with nothing to do, once invented for himself an occupation. Those about him, in his household and his village, were of the opinion that no such desperate step was necessary. He had an estate, and he was fond of hunting; these, they said, were occupation enough, and he should be content with the uneventful routines it imposed. But the gentleman was not content. And when he set out in earnest to live an altogether different life he was thought by everybody, first at home and then abroad, to be either strange or mad. He went away three times, returning once of his own accord but in the second and third cases being brought back by persons of the village who had pursued him for this purpose. He returned each time in an exhausted state, for the occupation he embraced was strenuous; and soon after his third homecoming he took to bed, made his will, confessed his sins, admitted that the whole enterprise had been an error, and died.

The gentleman who did these things would have remained utterly obscure had he not done them; and even then he would be unknown to fame had no history of him and them been written. But one was written, and it enjoys the reputation of being perhaps the best novel in the world. Not that its author ever speaks of it as fiction. He says it is history, or if you like biography; and he does not even claim credit for its composition. He merely translated it into Spanish from the Arabic original of one Cid Hamet. He assumes it to be true, but he made up none of its details, just as he had nothing to do with the grand conception—either the historian's conception of his subject or the subject's conception of himself. This last, of course, could never have been invented by another, least of all by any novelist. No, the truth about this gentleman is stranger than fiction can permit itself to be. If he had not lived he would never have been imagined. He did live, though, and here is his history.

The tale thus rescued from oblivion by Cervantes is both simple and mysterious. The sign of its simplicity is that it can be summarized in a few sentences. The sign of its mysteriousness is that it can be talked about forever. It has indeed been talked about as no other story ever was. For a strange thing happens to its readers. They do not read the same book. Or if they do, they have different theories about it. There were never so many theories about anything, one is tempted to say, as there are about *Don Quixote*. Yet it survives them all, as any masterpiece must do if it would live. A classic in the end must elude even its subtlest commentator. And so *Don Quixote* remains truer than anything that has been said or can be said about it. Nor is this doubted by those who know it best and love it most, though they may have their theories too. They are the most reluctant, because of their love, to discourse upon the essence of the book at the expense of its being, upon its idea rather than its life. It lives, they say, and has its being in all of the many words that make it up. They are beautiful words, and they have their own excuse for occurring where they do. Listen to them and you will have the life, at least the life; and after this it may turn out that nothing else will matter.

Let us do no less than that, and certainly no more, with the beginning of *Don Quixote*. Let us see what the words say, and let us try to have no theory about them. Sooner or later we may fail, but at the start it should be easy. And what do we hear Cervantes telling us? Not, for instance, that his hero thought himself to be something or someone other than the man he was. He suffered from no delusion as to his identity. It was merely that he had been reading many books, and out of them he formed a conception of life as he would henceforth live it if he could. He would live, that is to say, as knights once did in the romances of chivalry. His error, if error it was, consisted in taking these romances as history rather than as fiction; in believing, for example, that Amadis of Gaul himself had ever lived in the same sense that Julius Caesar did, or Charlemagne. Everybody in Spain read the romances, but nobody else believed them as this gentleman believed them. They had been written for fun, and they were to be read for fun. You finished one and you began another, and then you finished that; but there was no change in you except that you had been amused. But the logic of our gentleman, having a different premise, went on to a different conclusion. The life of a knight could be lived again. It even *should* be lived again, since the world now was in as bad a way as it had been in the time of Amadis.

And still he did not think he *was* a knight. He merely thought he could become one if he took the trouble. And he took much trouble, deliberately, step by conscious step. He changed his name to Don Quixote; it had been something like that before, but the new form struck him as better. He got together a suit of armor; he gave his old horse a name, Rozinante, that seemed fitting; and he decided upon a mistress. He had no mistress, but he took one in his mind and called her Dulcinea. Nor was she wholly imaginary. A neighbor girl, Aldonza Lorenzo, had been of interest to him once, without her knowing or caring that this was so. In any case she would do, as his bony horse would do, as his great-grandfather's rusty armor would do, and as his own new name would do. He was ready now to imitate the knights of old.

It is well to observe that imitation was his aim. Not impersonation, and not deception. Least of all would it be self-deception. He knew very well who he was. The only question was whether he would be able to act the part he had chosen. He was lean and strong, and so he might endure the necessary hardships. But could he think, feel, and above all talk like a knight? If he could not, then his self-education had been imperfect.

It had been good, however, in many branches of learning. He

could just as well have decided to live the life of a hermit or a saint, since he was proficient in the literature of devotion; or of a scholar, since his erudition was immense; or of a shepherd, since he had read and absorbed many pastorals. Indeed his niece, when he returned home the first time and it was deemed necessary to burn the romances that she, like the barber and the curate, supposed had made him mad, insisted that the pastorals in his library should be fed to the same flames, lest in the event of his being cured of his desire to be a knight he should "turn shepherd, and so wander through the woods and fields." She knew her uncle well. Perhaps she was not aware that he had once played with the idea of writing a romance of chivalry, or at any rate of completing one that had been left without an end. This was before the idea seized him of imitating in action the heroes of all such works. And if she had known she would scarcely have objected, since writing is a quiet occupation, done at a desk. But she did surely see the intensity inside the man: an intensity that might lead only God knew where, and maybe to the woods and fields.

His decision in favor of the knightly role was determined, we may think, by the very learning it entailed. The discipline of knighthood was to him the sum of all the arts and sciences; was wisdom itself; was a liberal education. Even before he became obsessed by the romances—an obsession so extreme that he sold pieces of his land to buy more books—he must have been distinguished for his erudition. His eloquence at all times, his acuteness as a critic, his marvelous memory for details out of the remotest authors mark him as a scholar, a man of intellect and sensibility. His power to fascinate others with his conversation is never questioned, least of all by the reader of the book whose hero he is. But he is most learned in the subject of romance. It has become his specialty; it has even grown into a pedantry. No other knight was ever so deeply versed in the philosophy of the game.

Amadis of Gaul, for instance, was no scholar. He was a great gentleman: "A man of few words, slowly provoked, and quickly pacified." And his romance still deserves its fame. It is simple, clear, and exciting, not to say excellently moral. We cannot disagree with the barber and the curate when they exempt it from the burning, nor can we think it too quaint that our own gentleman insists upon its hero's having lived and moved and had his being. "I dare almost say, I have seen Amadis of Gaul with these very eyes." We may have said the same thing about Hamlet, Falstaff, Achilles, Odysseus, Squire Western, and Pickwick; and may have wondered why others protested, though we refrained from calling them mad as Don Quixote did the Canon of Toledo because the Canon refused to believe in the existence of Amadis. Amadis was both courageous and gentle; his deportment at the court of the Emperor in Constantinople is the deportment of a man so witty and sweet of tongue that he can make us think of Dulcinea's lover. And as he went by several names—Beltenebros, The Knight of the Green Sword, The Greek Knight—so Don Quixote could become in turn The Knight of the Woeful Figure and The Knight of the Lions. Yet Amadis was no scholar. For one thing, he was "a man of few words." Don Quixote is Nestor by comparison. And one could scarcely say of Don Quixote that he was "slowly provoked" or "quickly pacified." Amadis was a beautiful animal, and as such he had the temperance for which we envy beasts. He did not have to talk about being a knight because he *was* a knight. Don Quixote, being at best an imitation knight, had of course to talk like one, but then he had—or he thought he had—to talk about the importance and virtue of doing so. And of acting the part so vehemently, on a stage containing no others of his kind, that the nature of his role could never be mistaken, even though this meant that he would have to be extravagant and rash.

And now a theory about him does emerge. It is that he was first and last an actor, a skillful and conscious actor, who wrote his own play as he proceeded and of course kept the center of its stage. "In my very childhood," he said once, "I loved shows, and have been a great admirer of dramatic presentations from my youthful days." "Plays," he told Sancho, are "the resemblance of realities," and deserve to be loved because "they are all instrumental to the good of the commonwealth, and set before our eyes those looking-glasses that reflect a lively representation of human life; nothing being able to give us a more just idea of nature, and what we are or ought to be, than comedians and comedies." This can remind us of Hamlet, his contemporary, who spoke of a mirror held up to nature, who had a weakness for theatricals, who himself is the best actor in his play, and who may or may not have been mad. We shall never know what Shakespeare thought about him on the last point, and we shall never know whether Cervantes held the theory held by every other person in his book, namely that the Don was mad: had forgotten who he was, did not know what he did, was literally deluded. Upon acquaintance, to be sure, he strikes everyone as sane on every subject other than knighthood; on arms, on art, on politics, on religion, on manners, on food and sleep. But on knighthood he is cracked. And even if there are those who might grant, if the question were raised, that he is only acting like a knight, they would still think it madness to do that. In a theater, yes; but this man does it on the highways of Spain, he makes the world his stage.

And right there is the crucial question. Supposing Don Quixote to have been in his initial conception of himself an actor and nothing but an actor, did he in fact forget that this was so, did he confuse the actor with the man, the stage with life, the pretense with reality? It is something like the question we ask about Hamlet: having decided to put on an "antic disposition" in order to deceive or reassure others, did he end by becoming infected with the germ of madness thus nursed in his imagination; or, to put it another way, is there any difference finally between the madman some think him and the intense, passionate, perilously overwrought and extremely perplexed person of genius whom anyone can recognize him as being? Either question is difficult to answer. But in Don Quixote's case it is not impossible to say that he does always know what he is doing; that he has his own reasons for what he does; and that if these would be nobody else's reasons, that is only because there is and was nobody quite like him in the world. He is that rare thing in literature, a completely created character. He is so real that we cannot be sure we understand him.

It is said of him on one occasion that he must be mad because he cannot help doing what he does. Carrasco and Cecial, who have gone after him to bring him home, and for their purpose have dressed as he is dressed in the accouterments of knighthood, suddenly look to themselves as mad as he. Or so it seems to Cecial, though Carrasco, having been educated at Salamanca, can say: "He that only plays the fool for his fancy may give over when he pleases," whereas the Don is condemned by insanity to play the fool forever. But that very Don will give over in the end; and until then it simply does not please him to do so. When the plowman who has rescued him from the tangle of his armor—he is on the way home, shortly after his first leaving it, to provide himself with money, clean shirts, and a squire (this will be Sancho)—when the plowman, his near neighbor, hears him calling himself Baldwin and Abindarez, he says to him that he is only "Senior Quexada"; and Don Quixote answers him with seven famous words. "I know very well who I am." This could mean, of course, that he knows he is Baldwin or Abindarez and therefore is mad. But it could also mean just what it says. It could mean in addition: "Very well, my man, I am doing what to your poor wit may seem a crazy thing, but I have my own reason and my own method, and your part is to pick me up without further argument or ado." Whatever it means, it is worthy of being remembered throughout the long book which in a sense it introduces. Halfway through that book its hero will say in exasperation: "Heaven knows my meaning." Perhaps only heaven does.

"All I aim at," he tells the barber midway in his career, "is only to make the world sensible how much they are to blame in not laboring to revive those most happy times in which the order of knight-errantry was in its full glory." This is after the barber has been telling him of a madman who thought himself Neptune. Don Quixote, rejecting the parallel, announces his actor's, his propagandist's aim; just as in the house of Don Diego he will implore young Don Lorenzo to consider "the vast advantages that would result" in the present age from the assistance of knights like those of old. Why shouldn't the thing be tried? He is always asking that question, even of those who doubt the actuality of knights in former ages. He is certain that they were actual, but even if they were not, the very idea of them, available now as then, is the idea that best expresses itself in the phrase "greatness of mind." Greatness of mind can exist again in those who cultivate it. His project is to cultivate a set of manners and actions that will make him look to outsiders like one who has the thing within him. The thing itself, however, is all that is ultimately important.

Seen in this aspect, Don Quixote has analogues at any time: the teacher who assumes maturity in his students and so gives them every thought he has; the gentleman whose manners consist in supposing that all other men are gentlemen too, and all women ladies; the statesman who takes it for granted that the people he rules are serious and can understand the best thing he can say; the poet who writes in the faith that his audience is no less subtle and profound, and no less wise, than himself. Such persons are often called, if not precisely mad, foolish for believing that the best can ever be. Or be again, in a world grown cynical and degenerate. Such a world doubts its own history: its Founding Fathers, say, were never what some sanguine people think they were. Yet one who can believe in them can imitate them now; and in so doing may become a statesman, and in that capacity restore the temper of a better time.

To speak like this is to put the best face on our hero, to make the most that can be made of his madness, if mad he was. He has a worst face, too, and it is high time to speak of that. He wears it when he does violence to harmless creatures who get in his way. We wince when he assaults the sheep, exclaiming that they are armies, and kills a number of them before he can be stopped. So with the funeral at night, with its strange torches which Cervantes deliberately makes beautiful so that we shall wince the more when Don Quixote, riding against them, works havoc among the mourners, one of whom even suffers a broken leg. We do not mind so much that he risks his own skin against windmills; that is his business, amusing to us or otherwise; but we do find him painful when he hurts people who in no sense deserve it. His acting now becomes extravagant with a vengeance; his role grows ruthless; he behaves more like a lunatic than like a knight; he is fanatical, as if he thought himself, like Providence, privileged to seem cruel. He lives by his own law, and does not disarm our criticism by doing great good in the end. He does no good to the boy whom the farmer is whipping; indeed, he only gets him whipped further as soon as his own back is turned. He does no good by freeing the galley slaves, or by beating monks and muleteers. And while we smile at the brilliant way he takes of saying he is above law and custom, we do not forget that insofar as he acts out such a part he is a maniac on the loose. As a knight, of course, he pays no bills for lodging or food. His motto is Pistol's: "Base is the slave that pays." Nor does he think he should ever be brought before a judge. "We are exempt from courts of judicature," he informs an officer of the Holy Brotherhood whose members are devoted to the task of ridding Spain's roads of its highwaymen, and indeed all Spain of its troublemakers. To the Brotherhood Don Quixote is himself a troublemaker, whatever claims he may make for himself as one who would rid the same country of its numerous evils. Here in other words is a rivalry between the law and one who says he *is* the law; and this rivalry, in the nature of things, never comes to an end. It cannot do so as long as Don Quixote keeps his faith and maintains his role.

He maintains it with astonishing ability. Sancho, for instance, thinking at the inn to escape without paying as his master had, is caught at the gate and tossed in a blanket. Sancho cannot carry the thing off; he is worse than a poor actor, he is no actor at all. He speaks what is on his mind, in accents that are native to him. And he feels sympathy when to do so is out of order. The knight he serves rarely demeans himself by making apologies for distressful things he has done. He may not be aware that he has caused distress; but even when it is called to his attention he keeps his head high, he is too lofty to ask people's pardons. His errors—for he does commit errors—have a way of coming home to his horizon; but he has a way of not seeing them there, or if he does, of explaining them away. He would give his attention to the whipped boy except for the fact that he is busy with a knight's duties: he must save the Princess Micomicona; so it is left to Sancho to comfort the poor lad. And it is customary with him to insist that even though he has injured somebody by mistake—which is to say, has mistaken him for something other than what he is—still, it was a good mistake, an honorable mistake, since it consisted only of misinterpreting appearances, and if the appearances had been in fact the reality he supposed them he was altogether to be praised for his forthright manner of attack.

He has succeeded at any rate in becoming at home in his role. The hostess of the inn who sees him as "a man of another world" is paying him the compliment that most would please him. He really does act and talk like an old-world man, with connections running clear back to the Age of Gold which he can so handsomely apostrophize. He has the language of this age at all times on his tongue, as he has its logic. It is no less essential, he tells Vivaldo, for knights to have ladies than for skies to have stars. Heine was to say the same thing centuries later, and in the same fashion to enjoy the figure:

> For with love there must be ladies,
> And the lady was as needful
> To the tuneful minnesinger
> As, to bread and butter, butter.

Who can doubt, listening to Don Quixote, that he knew he was eloquent and relished eloquence as an art? No knight in any romance ever talked more perfectly about his lady than this knight talks about Dulcinea, "lovely enemy of my repose." To imitate eloquence one must somehow share its inspiration. The Don can turn off his rhetoric when he has no need for it; he can sound like Sancho when he will. But when he would sound like Amadis of Gaul he can do that too.

Nor can we doubt the relish he takes in this. He is having a good time. So good a time that he develops a rich humor in himself. Notoriously he is laughed at, but he laughs too, and by no means always at others. On a certain morning when the sun shows him that it was fulling-mills, not giants, which he had heard the night before and summoned his courage to oppose, he laughs almost as heartily as Sancho does at the memory of the tall words he had cast upon the wind. Not quite as heartily, for Sancho overdoes it on his part, going even so far as to parody those words. "Am I, who am a Knight," thunders his master, "bound to know the meaning of every mechanic noise, and distinguish between sound and sound?" The question itself is delicious, and its asker knows it; just as he knows in Part II how to pull Sancho's leg by reciting the marvels he had met in the Cave of Montesinos—the marvels, mixed with such items as that he had blown his nose in the darksome cavern in order to make sure he was awake. His insistence in the Enchanted Bark that they have sailed thousands of miles is an answer to Sancho's statement that it is twenty years since they left La Mancha. His excellent relation with Sancho has rested all along upon a mutual understanding in which humor played its part. Did he expect Sancho to believe that an enchanter immobilized him so that he could do no more than gaze over the inn-yard wall as the squire got tossed in a blanket? Does he expect to be taken seriously when he speculates aloud that the voice under the ground—we know it is Sancho, fallen into a pit—is the voice of a soul in Purgatory? So much humor, so easily and so naturally expressed, is not the mark of a madman. It is not demonic humor; it is pleasantry, it is power and wisdom at play; and probably it is what makes Sancho love him so much that he can never leave him.

No reader forgets the Don's habit, formed early in the book, of explaining awkward occurrences by saying that enchanters have been busy: they have altered people's faces, they have caused objects to appear and disappear. It is a convenient device, and one's memory may not reach back to the moment of its conception. This seems to have been the moment when Don Quixote's housekeeper, asked where his study is, says, as she has been instructed: "What study?" For while he was in bed recovering from his first sally the door to the room where he kept his books had been removed and the wall plastered over. And the niece remarks that a conjurer or enchanter must be to blame. Why may it not be supposed that Don Quixote, always, like a good actor, alert to clues, saw at once the advantage of such a dodge, and determined to use it whenever it should come in handy? If so, it must have delighted him, when he called the windmills giants, to hear Sancho say: "What giants?" The trick would last him as long as he cared to use it—of course, with variations.

He will often find himself in the presence of other persons

who are acting parts, either to compete with him or to humor him into going home; or, as is sometimes the case, out of sheer roguery, for the sake of deceiving and cheating others. He will come through such competition with the highest honors; there is no actor in the book who is half so fine as he. The theatricals of Cardenio's friends are amateur by any just comparison—either, that is to say, the theatricals they habitually enact as ladies and gentlemen of fashion, or those they stage for what they suppose to be the benefit of the old madman they would hoodwink. There are many interesting ironies in the scene where Dorothea, claiming to be a damsel in distress, kneels before the mounted Knight and implores his help. One of these ironies is that she *is* distressed, as we have just learned by hearing her tell her tale of broken love; though of course we know that she is not the Princess Micomicona, in danger from a devilish giant. Another irony is there for her to measure when the Knight makes his first response. We do not know what she had expected to hear; certainly not these words that surpass in beauty the best she has ever read in any romance. Don Quixote had doubtless been represented to her by the barber and the curate as some sort of ancient fool who scarcely knows what he is babbling; but out of him comes a stream of words such as only great gentlemen can speak; and in his very manner there is "an awful grace and civility." She might well repent her decision to deceive so distinguished a person, mad or no. And here a third irony could lurk. For the Don may have labored toward just this result: her repentance, and beyond that her admiration at the skill with which he speaks his lines. How is one to know for sure that he believes her tale? It is well told, for she has read the romances and absorbed their style, and naturally he likes the way she tells it; but does he believe it? We shall never know, any more than we shall know whether the moving thanks he offers to the innkeeper's wife and her daughter and her maid when he leaves them to go home in the wooden cart are intended to strike them dumb with a sense of the injustice they have done him; or any more than we shall know, when he hangs by his hands outside the inn window, whether he wishes he had never got himself into such a pickle; or any more than we shall know in Part II whether he believes the Duke and the Duchess. More of them later; yet it is worth while to consider their castle as the best-appointed stage on which he ever acts; it contains his largest and most varied audience, and is the most opulent in its costumes and its lighting.

Don Quixote is rarely alone with us so that we may see what he would be like had he not an audience. If nobody else is with him, Sancho is. Yet Sancho does leave him once in the Black Mountain, when he goes off with the letter to Dulcinea, and we are not surprised to discover a conspicuous quiet in our hero's behavior. He no longer acts the madman. Left to himself, he is controlled and serene. In his own soul he may be always self-contained. As a private individual he does have his proper secrets—for example, he is modest, and will let none of the Duchess's maids undress him. Only Sancho may do that; and when Sancho goes off to govern his island he must do it by himself. Somehow this tells us volumes concerning a sanity he spends most of his days disguising.

And all the while there is that other role of shepherd ready to be assumed. He meets many goatherds, one of whom converses with his goats; he meets the beautiful Marcella, a girl of station who finds it convenient to dress like a shepherdess and roam the mountains about her home until the day arrives when she shall know which one of her many suitors she would marry; he is regularly reminded of the pastoral romances whose lovesick heroes he could imitate if it ever struck his fancy so to do. He holds the temptation off until the end, and even then it comes to nothing. The role of shepherd is less rich than that of knight. There is less learning in it, less depth, less morality, less metaphysic. He prefers the grand role that implies all other roles. He continues acting like a knight.

Nor does this need to mean that he merely pretends. To act as he acts is more than to ape; to imitate as he does is finally to understand. What is the difference between acting like a great man and being one? To act like a poet is to write poems; to act like a statesman is to ponder the nature of goodness and justice; to act like a student is to study; to act like a knight is to think and feel like one. When we tell a boy to act like a man we are not advising him to be dishonest. "Act well your part; there all the honor lies"—no one has ever detected cynicism in Pope's line. We even urge people to act natural, as if to be themselves required the exercise of art. And it does, as those unsure of themselves well know. All they have to do is to become sure; and then we shall say in praise of them that they are acting like themselves.

A mysterious region, this, and Don Quixote knows it to its utmost boundaries. If he did not—if he were nothing but a pretender, which is to say a poor actor—we should not be talking of him now. We are talking of him because we suspect that in the end he did become a knight. He thought his part through. Otherwise how could he have stunned the prostrate Dorothea with such words as these? "Rise, Lady, I beseech you; I grant you the boon which your singular beauty demands." And later on, how could he have stunned her again when he replied thus to her egregious flatteries? "No more, Madam, I beseech you. Spare me the trouble of hearing myself praised, for I mortally hate whatever may look like adulation; and though your compliments may deserve a better name, my ears are too modest to be pleased with any such discourse; 'tis my study to deserve and to avoid applause. All I will venture to say is, that, whether I have any valor or not, I am wholly at your service, even at the expense of the last drop of my blood." We can assume that Don Quixote spoke these lines as if he understood them, and spoke them with a corresponding beauty. But we must also remember that he composed them on the spot. He had no script. He was actor and playwright both. He was a hero made real as only the finest art achieves reality. And this in a book whose very problem is reality, a book which calls in question the existence of knights and the sanity of an obscure man who insisted that he could be one.

The world he walked and spoke in was a wonderful copy of the world that everybody knows, the world we think of every day as real. It has been justly said that no novel is more real than *Don Quixote*, and this is true even if we consider it without its hero. Cervantes placed him where all possible light could shine on the figure he cut. We tend to forget the author as we read, but we should pause occasionally to take note of the remarkable, the daring thing he has done. He has set a knight riding down Main Street, and of all merciless places, in Spain. It had been relatively easy for the authors of the romances to make their knights attractive. Given a willingness in their readers to find the spectacle pleasing, all they had to do was to fill the landscape with armored men who had no other occupation than that of fighting for their ladies—who, waiting in their castles, had no other need than to be beautiful and anxious day by day. Chivalry by this account was a day-dream, shared in a conspiracy of pretense by author and reader alike, and the world it took place in was not required to contain such gritty essences as peasants on their mules, artisans at their lathes, traders at their desks, or thieves and beggars in the back streets of cities. It was not expected that dust or wind should be present, or money, or charity, or filth, or such kinds of food as crusts of bread, lumps of cheese, and slices of raw onion. And the result even then was a charming literature, as Cervantes knows as well as his hero, and as well as every other person in the story. Even the hard-headed house-keeper, at home in La Mancha, wants to sprinkle her master's books with holy water to exorcise the sorcery in them. Yet it had not been a real literature as Cervantes, starting to write his masterpiece, comprehended the term. Into this masterpiece he would put everything he knew, all that he smelled as well as all that he thought and imagined.

And upon every item of his account he bestowed the dignity of an incomparable style. The stream of his words is beautiful and strong, nor does it object to any article it is called upon to float toward its natural destination. All things, all persons, ride the current of this world as if they had a right to do so. Cervantes once calls the work he pretends to be translating a "grave, high-sounding, minute, soft, and humorous history." Grave and humorous: it is comedy at its best, with everything remembered out of life, and with all things in it weighted equally, justly. And because of that equal weight, nothing feels heavier than it should, neither the fine knight on Rozinante nor the plain people who stare at him and doubt that he is as fine as he says he is. There is a lightness in the book that makes every reader love it as he loves his own mind. It is both vast and delicate, both formidable and buoyant. The writer of it—we can never doubt this—was happy as he wrote.

He must have been happiest when his hero, come home to provide himself with a squire, thought of his neighbor Sancho and persuaded him to go along. There has never been a better device for fiction than this of two men who see the same things but consider them differently. And so just is Cervantes, so equal in his love, that neither of them is ever at a disadvantage in our view. Each is a created individual, with a world of his own which the other must accept—not approve, but certainly accept, as if it had as much right to exist and be believed in as his own. Each calls the other names; each accuses the other of being mad; they quarrel, they fall out and are silent for long stretches; they insist they do not understand each other. Yet their mutual love increases until at last they are, as others say, one man.

"Do you know where you are?" cries Don Quixote in the castle of the Duke when Sancho has disturbed decorum by insisting that Dapple, his ass, be suitably stabled and fed. "Every man," says Sancho, "must tell his wants, be he where he will. Here I bethought myself of Dapple, and here I spoke of him. Had I called him to mind in the stable, I would have spoken of him there." He has only one language, the language of the Panzas, and he uses it as language was intended to be used, to make known the thought within. Don Quixote is master of many languages, just as he is master of many thoughts, and he inhabits as it were a variety of worlds, though all of them may be one world, his world, in the end. But Sancho inhabits *this* world and no other; and he inhabits it so simply that he becomes, both for Cervantes and for us who are looking on, its perfect symbol. Don Quixote does not merely ride through this world; he takes it with him, he looks at it and listens to it every day, he sleeps and feeds with it, he argues with it, he fights with it and makes up, he accepts it always as being there. Nor does it ever change. Stubbornly, it is what it is, as he is too. The Don and the Squire never convince each other, even though they take a greater and greater pleasure in adventuring side by side.

Each of them, too, has a household out of which he comes;

the reality of both is documented. Don Quixote has no wife and children, but we shall not forget his niece, his housekeeper, and his neighbors, for they go with him even though he thinks he has left them behind; unique as he is among them, he still cannot be separated from them any more than the heart can be removed from the body, or the sting from the bee. Sancho Panza has of course his own family, nor does he ever want to forget the wife and daughter he has been persuaded to abandon. They are not really abandoned. They are constantly, and sometimes guiltily, in his thoughts. The sense of guilt is not perhaps complete in Sancho; if it were, he would make good his frequent threats of going home. It is often no more than an excuse for blaming his master. "See," says the squire, "how you plucked me out of the bosom of my family, and all for this"—a tossing in a blanket, a beating by a rogue. Yet he does miss his little house and the people in it who are so much like him. Twice they rejoice to see him coming home over the hill outside the village, and twice he rejoices with them. And when he is governing his island nothing gives him more satisfaction than such a letter as this from Teresa his wife, with news in it of Sanchica his daughter:

"The news here is, that Berrueca has married her daughter to a sorry painter that came hither, pretending to paint anything. The township set him to paint the King's arms over the Town Hall. He asked 'em two ducats for the job, which they paid him. So he fell to work, and was eight days a-daubing, but could make nothing of it at last; and said he could not hit upon such piddling kind of work, and so gave 'em their money again. . . . Pedro de Lobo's son has taken orders, and shaved his crown, meaning to be a priest. Minguilla, Mingo Silvato's grand-daughter, heard of it, and sues him upon a promise of marriage; ill tongues do not stick to say she has been with child by him, but he stiffly denies it. We have no olives this year, nor is there a drop of vinegar to be got for love or money. A company of soldiers went through this place, and carried along with them three wenches out of the town. I don't tell thee their names, for mayhaps they will come back, and there will not want some that will marry 'em, for better for worse. Sanchica makes bone-lace, and gets her three half-pence a day clear, which she saves in a box with a slit, to go towards buying household stuff. The fountain in the market is dried up. A thunderbolt lately fell upon the pillory—there may they all light. I expect thy answer to this. Heaven send thee long to live, longer than myself, or rather, as long; for I would not willingly leave thee behind me in this world. Thy wife, Teresa Panza."

The reality of this is not the only reality in *Don Quixote*, but it is perhaps the basic one; it is the ground on which all other realities stand. And it is firm ground, built there by hands that know of what minerals the earth was originally composed. Nor is it laid down with condescension or disgust. Cervantes respects the world his people walk on, however high or low they hold their heads. Not the least of his triumphs is that he manages neither to satirize nor to idealize his so-called common people. They seem to be exactly what they ought to be: the people of this world, for better or for worse, with no doubt in their heads that they should exist and respect themselves. Merely to hear them talking makes one happier, more reassured, than one knows how to say. As when, for a final instance, the innkeeper's wife and daughter are attending to Don Quixote's bruises. The bruises were inflicted by cudgels, but Sancho, to save his master's dignity, not to speak of his own, since he was cudgeled too, has told the women they were the result of a fall from the top of a high rock. "And by the way," says he, "I beseech you save a little of that same tow and ointment for me too, for I don't know what's the matter with my back, but I fancy I stand mainly in want of a little greasing too." "What, I suppose you fell too," says the landlady. "Not I," says Sancho, "but the very fright that I took to see my master tumble down the rock has so wrought upon my body that I'm as sore as if I had been sadly mauled." "It may well be as you say," puts in the daughter; "for I have dreamed several times that I have been falling from the top of a high tower without ever coming to the ground; and when I have waked, I have found myself as out of order, and as bruised, as if I had fallen in good earnest." Meanwhile Maritornes, the entirely illiterate maid of the inn, has been holding a candle so that her mistress could see the Don. "How do you call this same gentleman?" she asks the squire. "He's Don Quixote de La Mancha," replies Sancho, "and he is a knight-errant, and one of the primest and stoutest that ever the sun shined on." "A knight-errant," cries the wench. "Pray, what's that?"

## 2

"A knight-errant," cried Maritornes. "Pray, what's that?" If Don Quixote, groaning under his bruises, had heard her put the question he might have had more reason to despair than normally he had. Not that he was subject to despair; he was indeed well armed against it; but here was a worse thing than the incredulity he had so far found. Here was pure ignorance: Maritornes, judging by her words, had never even heard of the profession he was trying to restore. Later it turned out not to be quite so bad as that: the wench had read some of the romances, or had had them read to her, and she was eager to testify that they pleased her. "For my part," she said, "I think there are mighty pretty stories in those books, especially that one about the young lady who is hugged under the orange tree, when the damsel watches lest somebody comes, and stands with her mouth watering all the while; and a thousand such stories, which I would often forego my dinner and supper to hear." But now not so. "Pray, what *is* a knight-errant?" It could have appeared to Don Quixote that his duty henceforth was not only to bring back knighthood but to create it out of nothing, to make something be that never was. He might not mind so much that someone thought him mad for dressing the part in this late day and age, for such a person at least recognized the part; and subsequently, when he heard the Gentleman in the Green Coat exclaim, staring at his armor, that he would never have believed a knight could exist in the present world had he not seen this one now, the Don, however much he doubted the sobriety of the remark, would be able to take comfort in the knowledge it implied. Here, though, was the stone wall of illiteracy, to charge which might seem even to Don Quixote, weary on the innkeeper's bed, a project so hopeless of success that the mere idea of undertaking it must certainly be mad.

But there is no suggestion that he heard Maritornes. And in any case he was halfway through a series of encounters with madness which Cervantes, his creator, could not have wished to terminate; and happily so, for the series is most edifying, and manages, like several other series of adventures in the book, to throw a fascinating light upon the identity, the character, and the inward thinking of the Don.

Not long before this the knight and his squire, fleeing into a mountain wilderness to escape the Holy Brotherhood, had come upon "a man that skipped from rock to rock, over briars and bushes, with wonderful agility. He seemed naked from the waist upwards, with a thick black beard, his hair long and strangely tangled, his head, legs, and feet bare; on his hips a pair of breeches that appeared to be of sad-colored velvet, but so tattered and torn that they discovered his skin in many places." The fellow, in short, gave every appearance of being deranged; though a goatherd came by to say that a few months ago he was not at all like this. He was handsome and well-dressed. But he had penetrated these mountains with the intention, as it were, of deranging himself. And soon enough he emerged from his fastness to caper and rage and beat whatever men he came upon; also, he moaned from time to time about a certain Ferdinand who had betrayed him. Clearly it was a love madness, complicated to be sure by some sense of guilt which induced him to do penance for a great sin of his own commission. Now Don Quixote could not but be vastly interested in a phenomenon so reminiscent of the romances, where many a knight had gone through just such trials of the spirit, usually in despair over some misunderstanding between him and his mistress, or perhaps some act of infidelity on her part. Amadis of Gaul, soon to change his name to Beltenebros, had so suffered on account of Oriana; and Orlando's famous madness had been so motivated by Angelica. It was necessary, therefore, to meet this man, who to be sure was not in the costume of a knight but who did one of the things all knights had done. Perhaps he needed help in his distress, and would particularly appreciate the help of one schooled in his condition.

The strange fellow, whom we hear called the Knight of the Mountain and the Knight of the Wood, though we shall learn that he is Cardenio, a young man of fashion, of course puts in his appearance almost at once, and after a moment of amazement over what he sees in the person of our hero does to be sure commence a sequence of strange acts. He consents to tell his story on the promise of Don Quixote not to interrupt it. It concerns Don Ferdinand, as we might have expected, but it also concerns his own mistress, Lucinda, and another lady whom we are eventually to know, when we see all these persons in the flesh, as Dorothea. The story proceeds without interruption until it reaches the remark that "Lucinda, who took great delight in reading books of knight-errantry, desired me to lend her the romance of *Amadis de Gaul*." Now Don Quixote can restrain himself no longer; he breaks into a eulogy of his favorite literature, and thereby brings the tale to a close; though the stranger who was telling it trails off with the cryptic observation: "I am positively convinced, nor shall any man in the world persuade me to the contrary, and he is a blockhead who says, that great villain Elisabet never lay with Queen Madasima." Those two persons in *Amadis of Gaul* have not been mentioned heretofore, nor are they relevant now; but the Don is so sure that Madasima has been maligned that he defends her "as if she were his true and lawful princess," and is struck for this by a great stone which the madman picks up and throws at him. A fracas follows, and even Sancho is involved; but then the madman runs away and it is some time before we know the rest of his story, not to say before we meet the characters in it.

Is he a veritable madman, as by contrast Don Quixote suddenly seems not to be? He is not a knight, nor does he pretend to be one. He does, we can think, pretend to be out of his head. And for all we know, Don Quixote thinks this too, though of that we cannot be altogether certain. He may suspect as we do that Cardenio, unhappy in love, has resorted to an extreme expression of the state: extreme either because he is actually all but crazy with grief or because for some odd reason he wishes to appear so—possibly because he too has read the romances and now seeks an artist's satisfaction in the imitation of their heroes. The only difference between Don Quixote and ourselves would be that the spectacle gives him pleasure: again, an artist's pleasure, not merely in a pretty good performance but in the cue it offers for a better performance by himself.

For as he and Sancho ride on he announces that he will do penance in these same mountains, here and now, for Dulcinea. He will imitate the imitator of Beltenebros and Orlando. He will put on a show that would not shame Orlando if he were present to behold it. He has done many things the knights did, but not this one; through an oversight he has neglected to stage their best, their sure-fire scene. Not that he speaks in terms of shows and scenes; he urges an inner necessity, and in doing so bewilders Sancho, who is not aware of anything that Dulcinea could have done to pain her lover or of anything that her lover has failed to do for her honor and glory. As for Cardenio, says Sancho, "who but a madman would have minded what a madman said," about Madasima or anything? As for Dulcinea, the very thought of penance is preposterous. There is nothing to go mad *about*. "What lady has sent you a packing, or so much as slighted you? When did you ever find that my lady Dulcinea del Toboso did otherwise than she should do, with either Moor or Christian?" "Why," cries Don Quixote, "there's the point. In this consists the singular perfection of my undertaking; for, mark me, Sancho, for a knight-errant to run mad upon any just occasion is neither strange nor meritorious; no, the rarity is to run mad without a cause, without the least constraint or necessity." He will, in other words, go ritually mad; he will do it in cold blood—or, to use his own words, in the dry rather than the wet; and then Dulcinea will know what he could have done had she given him sufficient reason. Oh, he will not do what Orlando did: tear up trees by the roots, slay shepherds, destroy flocks, burn houses, and all of that. It is more likely that he will take Beltenebros for his model, and merely lament in verse.

But first he unsaddles his steed and sends him off, for he

must do his penance in the extremity of want. "Go, Rozinante," he intones with his usual felicity, "he that hath lost his freedom gives thee thine." And then he announces precisely what his program is. He will tear off his clothes, knock his head against the rocks, and do other things too which Sancho must stay to see. But Sancho cannot bear the thought, particularly of the rocks. Find something softer, he suggests: water, or cotton. Don Quixote thanks him for his concern, but assures him that "these seeming extravagancies are no jests. Far from it, they must be performed seriously and solemnly; for otherwise we should transgress the laws of chivalry, that forbid us to tell lies upon the pain of degradation. Now to pretend to do one thing, and effect another, is an evasion which I esteem to be as bad as lying. Therefore the blows which I must give myself on the head ought to be real, substantial, sound ones, without any trick or mental reservation; for which reason I would have thee leave me some lint and salve." The upshot of it all is that Sancho only sees his master stripped upward to the waist and turning two cartwheels; then he is off, and Don Quixote proceeds to the relatively quiet occupation of composing a melancholy poem on the subject of his grief.

How mad is he to insist on acting such a part? For now he is clearly acting; he says so, and even Sancho believes it, though Sancho wonders why anyone should want to punish himself this way. Our wonder is perhaps less strong, for we know Don Quixote better. Yet what is it that we know? And what is the result in our minds of the more or less unconscious comparison we make of Don Quixote with Cardenio, not to speak of Anselmo in the tale of *The Curious Impertinent* which the host of the next inn will read from a manuscript left with him by its author? Anselmo is really mad; any psychologist would say so; but he is only in a story. The story was written by Cervantes, as all of *Don Quixote* was; and through all of *Don Quixote* the question will be asked, or perhaps only suggested, whether its hero is more mad or less mad than somebody else. The final answer may be that he seems somehow more intelligible than most of his companions in the narrative, and somehow more natural. But it will remain a question to which Cervantes will appear to say he has no answer. It will simply continue to be asked, in a series of situations that, considered as a series, will run through the entire work like a thread—or better yet, like an artery conducting life to its remotest parts.

A second such series runs its course among incidents whose bearing is upon the great, central question of the book: What is reality? It is the most famous question in the world, though here it takes many forms. How real were the knights in the old books; and if they were not real, what does it mean to say that the books seem real as we read them? This is something like the question of what we mean when we say of a play that it is real. We know it is not; we have gone into a dark building to see it acted out in circumstances that no one needs to tell us are artificial; and the actors are artists, are imitators—no question of that. But when we like what they do we call it real; we even call it natural, though we have not forgotten that it is art. A set of persons brought in off the street and asked to live their lives on that same stage would seem by comparison unreal; or at the best, sub-real. And so as to the hero of this book. How real is his belief that he either is or can become a knight? He never appears to expect that anybody will mistake him for Amadis of Gaul. He is only Amadis in modern times. Or *like* Amadis—which? And for that matter, what of the numerous persons in the story who are masked or disguised, or if not literally that, then playing parts for another kind of purpose than the Don's? What is the reality in their case?

And how real, too, are the tales of love and adventure which Cervantes interpolates from time to time? At the beginning of Part II he will permit the opinion to be expressed, by certain readers of Part I, that there were too many such narratives in it; too much fiction diluted the pure history which it would otherwise have been. An equivalent question would be this: How real, which is to say how lifelike and convincing, are those tales? And how do they compare with the novel that contains them? For the comparison is more than suggested; it is inevitable. We have not only the tales, but in one case, Cardenio's, we have the persons of it appear so that we can listen to them talking like themselves, which is to say like the conventional lovers of romance—not old but new romance, not the romance of ladies and knights but that of ladies and gentlemen. The tales are told by a master of narrative—nobody ever told stories better than Cervantes—but is he not still more a master in the whole? And does not his battered old hero look and sound more real when he reappears upon the scene, even in his outlandish metal clothes, than the mannikins who do not recognize his humanity and would dismiss him from the species if they could? The question keeps putting itself; and never more sharply perhaps than it is put on one occasion by the Don himself, when, seated at the inn table with Dorothea and the rest, he exclaims: "What mortal in the world, at this time entering within this castle, and seeing us sit together as we do, will imagine and believe us to be the same persons which in reality we are?" He means by reality in his own case the knighthood he has assumed, just as he thinks the inn to be a castle. But as for the inn, has it not begun to look more like a castle than an inn, seeing that the most marvelous meetings have taken place within its halls? It has become a crossroads of recognition, a citadel of romance; at least the four lovers think of it that way, as well as does our eminently happy Don, who will have less reason henceforth to insist that inns are castles; they are castles anyhow.

The series is as long as the book; indeed it makes the book; but it may be worth while to remove a segment of it and consider what we find among its members. The best segment for the purpose is in Part II, and begins with Sancho. The knight and the squire have left home again, and their first destination is Toboso, of which Dulcinea is lady and queen. As they approach the village, each makes it clear to the other that he has never seen the peerless dame; but no matter, now they will; though when they are indeed there Don Quixote finds out a retreat in a neighboring grove where he can wait with dignity while Sancho goes with a message and—hopefully—brings back one. But Sancho conceives a stratagem. "Now then," he tells himself, "my master being so very mad as to mistake sometimes one thing for another, black for white and white for black, I guess 'twill be no hard matter to pass upon him the first country wench I shall meet with for the Lady Dulcinea. If he won't believe it, I'll swear it; so that when he finds I won't flinch he'll either resolve never to send me on more of his sleeveless errands, or he'll think some one of those wicked wizards has transmogrified her into some other shape out of spite." And so it goes. Having discovered three ill-favored wenches riding out from town on three young asses, he hurries to make his master meet them, promising that one of them is Dulcinea, peerless in grace and beauty, and that the other two are damsels who attend her. Yet Don Quixote, gazing at them with the best will in the world, sees "nothing but three wenches upon as many asses."

Sancho had supposed he would believe anything. But he does not believe this; except that he goes on to say that base enchanters must have labored to deprive him of the happiness of seeing the object of his wishes "in her natural shape and glory," with the result that he is now "the most unfortunate man in the universe." Sancho, who will pay heavily for the deception he has practiced, at the moment is overjoyed by the way his predictions have worked out. He does not seem to feel the change that we as readers now feel to be coming over the world he traverses with his master. The Don's senses, supposing that they ever have deceived him, will deceive him less and less; which means that his mind will have more and more to do, either in the hypothecation of necromancers or in the puzzling out of identities which at first blush are hard to see; or, beyond either of those exercises for his wit, in the devising of mysteries with which to confound the sensible Sancho. More and more, that is to say, Don Quixote's humor will appear. Henceforth he is less the violent than the ingenious knight, set down in subtler circumstances and called upon to solve complexer problems.

The two men ride on, and what should cross the road ahead of them but a cart driven by the Devil, who has for fellow passengers an angel, an emperor, a knight, and several other remarkable personages. Don Quixote, who in Part I might have charged them, merely challenges them to state their business in the world; and upon being told that they are strolling players who perform a piece called "The Parliament of Death," relaxes and smiles. "Now by the faith of my function," he says, "I find we ought not to give credit to appearances before we have made the experiment of feeling them." Again, that is to say, his senses do not deceive him; or if they have done so, he accepts the ready explanation: these are paid actors who because of their costumes look like other persons than those they are. There is a little trouble with the troupe, but soon enough he goes on with Sancho, saying: "Let us leave these idle apparitions, and proceed in search of more substantial and honorable adventures." He has shuffled his lenses; he is playing games with optics; he is even juggling mirrors.

And then he meets the *Knight* of the Mirrors. That evening, as he dozes with Sancho in the open air, he is awakened by the voice of a man in armor who dismounts from his horse and addresses another man who is certainly, judging by appearances, his squire. Here in the very world which hitherto has known no other knight than Don Quixote is one who furthermore will profess to be his enemy; for when the four men talk, knight with knight and squire with squire, the stranger is impertinent enough to claim that he has vanquished in battle no less a hero than Don Quixote de La Mancha. That cannot be, roars the true Don Quixote; it must have been someone like him, though few living men are like him; it could not have been Don Quixote, he at last declaims, for I am he. So the next morning there must be an encounter between them, with both agreeing that the winner may impose his will upon the loser. The strange knight dresses for the fray in armor decorated with little looking-glasses in the shape of half-moons; they ride, they meet; and the stranger falls. As he falls he discloses the face of the Bachelor Sampson Carrasco; and the squire soon confesses that he is Cecial. We learn from a subsequent conversation between the two that they have followed Don Quixote and Sancho in this guise with the expectation of securing their return home; Carrasco of course would win the encounter and then announce his will: that Don Quixote should go back to his village.

As for Don Quixote himself, has he not had a very complicated adventure? Instead of needing to pretend that some gentleman he met was a knight, he has met what seemed to be a veritable knight, and one furthermore who had heard of *him.* And if in our view the stranger is interesting because he is not like one of the strolling players, an actor by profession, yet nevertheless is one man acting as if he were another—a man, shall we say, who is acting like an actor—Don Quixote entertains no such view, or at any rate he acts as if he didn't. He insists as usual that an enchanter has been busy. He says to the warrior on the ground: "I do confess and believe, that though you seem to be the Bachelor Sampson Carrasco, you are not he, but some other whom my enemies have transformed into his resemblance, to assuage the violence of my wrath and make me entertain with moderation the glory of my victory."

No sooner do we confess that we are staggered by the complexity which the series has attained than we are called upon to witness the episode of the lions. Don Quixote, who formerly saw *A* as *B* (windmills as giants), in time saw *A* as *A* (wenches as wenches) in spite of Sancho's directions that he see them otherwise. Then, seeing *A* once more as *B* (the players as devil and angel), he was quickly persuaded that the one impersonated the other; though it was more difficult to see behind the disguise of Carrasco the Carrasco who was really there, so that Don Quixote could assert that *B* was *B* even though wizards made it appear that *B* was *A*. Now, traveling with the Gentleman in the Green Coat, he encounters a wagon bearing in cages two lions who not only look fierce but are certified by their keeper to be fierce. The Don forthwith resolves to prove his courage by standing before the door of the male lion's cage, which he commands the keeper to open, and taking whatever comes. It is not his fault that the male lion, a truly formidable beast, "after he had looked about him a while, turned his tail, and having showed Don Quixote his posteriors, very contentedly lay down again in his compartment." Don Quixote orders the keeper to prod him with his pole; but the keeper has had enough proof of the old man's courage, which he promises forever to extol. "Well, Sancho," says the Don, "what dost thou think of this? Can enchantment prevail over true fortitude? No, these magicians may perhaps rob me of success, but never of my invincible greatness of mind." Not only has he demonstrated his lack of fear; he has undergone a further refinement in the series we are witnessing. He has seen

*A* as *A* (lions as lions, and dangerous beyond a doubt), only to discover that they have been changed inside their skins; though he has not been changed inside of his, where he was and is more courageous than the lookers-on supposed, since they had seen him only as a man, and could not foresee that he would have, hidden within him, the heart of a lion. Small wonder that he goes henceforth by the title Knight of the Lions.

And then there is the business of Basil and Quiteria, two lovers who are not permitted to marry. But Basil at the wedding plays a clever trick and gets his Quiteria after all. Pretending to resign her to the rich Camacho who has spread a feast for the many guests who have come (they include Sancho, who for once fills his belly to bursting), he falls on his sword and welters on the ground in what appears to be his own blood. With what sounds like his last breath he asks the curate in charge to marry him and Quiteria; and Camacho is willing enough to assume that he shall have her a few minutes hence as a widow in name only. But as soon as the ceremony is performed, "up starts Basil briskly from the ground, and with an unexpected activity whips the sword out of his body, and catches his dear Quiteria close in his arms." A miracle, cries the multitude; but it was only a stratagem. "The curate came with both hands to feel the wound, and discovered that the sword had nowhere passed through the cunning Basil's body, but only through a tin pipe full of blood artfully fitted."

Here is another actor, playing in real life a part which gets for him the thing he wants. Carrasco failed, but Basil has succeeded—with simpler means, too, for all he had to supply was a tin tube full of blood. There is a battle, of course, and of course Don Quixote, who has been a fascinated observer, enters it on the side of the ingenious contriver. Perhaps he would have done so in any case, since love is his prime concern; yet he would have every admiration for so fine an actor as Basil. He will enjoy other encounters with mimes, notably that with Master Peter's puppet show. But enough of the series has been seen to make it seem indeed a series, searching in its conception and bewildering in its variety. It should not seem strange that as our hero experiences it in all of its involutions he grows steadily more abstracted, and even sad. He has much to think about. The world is full of actors, and he must study his role as he never studied it before.

A third series, and the last to be examined, is longer than either of the first two and perhaps more famous; yet it is so closely interwoven with them both, and particularly with the second, that it is difficult to isolate and discuss alone. It is the series of hoaxes, or pretended agreements on the part of others that Don Quixote is what he says he is, which comes to a climax in the grand deception by the Duke and the Duchess. It complicates the career of the hero and at the same time prolongs it. Again and again he might have returned home by his own choice had not success appeared to attend his efforts. It was, alas, an illusory success; he never was able to deceive or convince anybody; but the illusion gave him courage to go on.

His very first success was a little one, scarcely recognizable as such. He got away from home without anyone's stopping him, by "the private door of his backyard," whence he rode into the fields "wonderfully pleased to see with how much ease he had succeeded in the beginning of his enterprise," which of course must be a secret from the women who till now had run his life. His next success was greater because it solved a pressing need; he must be dubbed a knight, and the keeper of the first inn he stopped at humored him by going through the necessary motions. Also, he won out there against the muleteers who would throw his armor out of the horse-trough while he was holding vigil over it. Now he felt truly successful, so that his unhorsing of the monk and his triumph over the Biscayan, not to say his undisputed championship of Marcella against those who would pursue her, and his managing to get out of the second inn without paying for food or lodging, could seem to fall in with a pattern already established. Nothing would stop him now. Even Vivaldo, the gentleman who became interested in him at the funeral of Marcella's unhappy lover, indulged him by consenting to discuss with him the philosophy of knighthood; he actually paid him the compliment of arguing with him concerning the relative merits of knights and friars.

There is scarcely a moment from this point on when someone is not humoring, indulging, or hoaxing the Knight of the Woeful Figure. The motives may be many—to make him seem more foolish than ever, to escape from his uplifted arm, to create amusement in a world which has too little of that, to maneuver him back home—but the technique tends not to vary. His primary premise or assumption is accepted: he is what he says he is, and the world is what he seems to think it. Men discourse with him as if they believed his own remarks made sense, and maidens who consider him an old fool serenade him as if they really hoped to steal his affections away from Dulcinea. Perhaps there is no time when somebody could not have got him home quite simply, by the use of force. He is strong and clever, but he is not a giant, and enough stout arms could have subdued him, surely. But such is not the way of the world in which Cervantes has placed him. It is possible to suppose that he interests the inhabitants of that world more deeply than they admit or even know. And their hoaxes may tell us at least as much about themselves as about the intended victim. It is almost as if they wanted him to keep the fiction up. Certainly their devices strengthen his desire to do so. The success he seems to have makes him more sanguine still; pours oil, not water, on the flame.

And the trouble they take to fool him! The barber and the curate spend as much time away from home as he does, and make themselves far more uncomfortable. Their effort balances in the first part the all but incredible effort in Part II of the Duke and the Duchess. They give as much thought to Don Quixote as they would have given to a genuine knight, and furthermore, by enlisting the aid of Dorothea and her friends, they recruit as it were the entire population of the book into the service of proving that he should have done what he did in the first place. Nor can they and the Holy Brotherhood get him home at last without "enchanting" him into the wooden cart that takes him there. It is a curious spectacle: the savior of the world in a country vehicle. And Don Quixote makes much of this, musing aloud so that Sancho may hear: "Among all the volumes of chivalry that I have turned over, I never read before of knights-errant drawn in carts, or tugged along so leisurely, by such slothful animals as oxen. For they used to be hurried along with prodigious speed, enveloped in some dark and dusky cloud, or in some fiery chariot drawn by winged griffins, or some such expeditious creatures. But I must confess, to be drawn thus by a team of oxen, staggers my understanding not a little; though perhaps the enchanters of our times take a different method from those in former ages." But a spectacle no less curious is the escort he has with him somewhat as whales have schools of little fishes in their wake. Men ride up and down, before and after the cart, as if it contained an important person. And if Don Quixote, knowing who he is, knows also who they are, though he maintains that he does not, he is having his own huge joke at their expense, however comfortless the journey is.

The time comes in Part II, after the diverting incident of Basil and Quiteria, when Don Quixote conceives a hoax of his own. There is no other plausible explanation of what happens at the Cave of Montesinos, which our hero, who is quite as inquisitive as Odysseus, has heard about and is delighted to find in his path. Nothing will do but that he shall descend into it as Odysseus himself went down to Hades, or as Dante went through Hell. He and Sancho have picked up a wandering scholar who waits above ground with the terrified squire while his master explores the recesses of the earth. The preparations are deliberate and delightful. The Don is to be let down on a rope by which Sancho and the scholar will at a signal pull him up when his investigations are done. One thing, however, disturbs the Don. "We did ill," he says, "not to provide ourselves of a little bell, that I could have carried down with me, to ring for more or less rope as I may have occasion for, and inform you of my being alive." This does not reassure Sancho, nor is it intended to. But after prayers to the absent Dulcinea, down goes her intrepid lover, talking as he goes, until his voice is drowned in the windings of the cave and all the cordage is run out. "That done, they began to consider whether they should hoist him up again immediately or no. However, they resolved to stay half an hour, and then they began to draw up the rope; but were strangely surprised to find no weight upon it; which made them conclude, the poor gentleman was lost. Sancho, bursting out in tears, made a heavy lamentation, and fell a hauling up the rope as fast as he could, to be thoroughly satisfied. But after they had drawn up about fourscore fathoms, they felt a weight again, which made them take heart; and at last they plainly saw Don Quixote."

Yet when they get him up he is in a trance, and time must pass before he can tell what he has seen in the lateral passage he explored, abandoning the rope till he returned and needed it again. What he says he saw—undoubtedly the trance has given him leisure to invent details—astounds Sancho not merely because it contains so many wonders out of old romance but chiefly because it involves a vision of Dulcinea; and not the Dulcinea of Don Quixote's customary description but the very wench whom Sancho showed him near Toboso. She is enchanted, of course, as Sancho had known his master would think. Sancho's idea has come home to roost, and he will have to live with it. He does, throughout the rest of the book, with pain and much chagrin. But was she really down there? He will keep asking, and will never find out; or at least for a long time he won't. Now *he* has been hoaxed, and by a man who if he is as mad as most people think him would hardly be capable of the jest. And Sancho will be hoaxed again in the Enchanted Bark. But the hoax of all hoaxes will be awaiting them both as they approach the domain of the Duke.

First they meet the Duchess as she hunts with her company in an open field: "A very fine lady upon a white pacing mare, in green trappings, and a saddle of cloth of silver. The lady herself was dressed in green, so rich and gay that nothing could be finer." Don Quixote sends Sancho forward to convey his respects, and Sancho is not too much surprised to learn that both the Duchess and her husband, who is hunting in another field, know very well who these men are; they have read about them in Part I, and in fact the Duchess recognizes them both without difficulty. She will send for the Duke while the Don comes up. This happens; the most exquisite courtesies are exchanged; and the famous knight is invited to the castle. For its owners have had time to confer, and Cervantes tells us that they were "resolved, as long as he stayed with them, to give him his own way, and humor him in all things, treating him still with all the forms essential to the entertainment of a knight-errant; which they were the better able to do, having been much conversant with books of that kind." They embark, that is to say, upon a program of pretense which will consume all of their time and much of their wealth for weeks to come, and which will inspire before it is ended the remark that they must be madder than the gentleman they hoax.

However that may be, the Duke sees to it on this first day that when Don Quixote arrives at the castle he is met "by two lackeys or grooms in long vests, like nightgowns, of fine crimson satin." They hail him as "Great and mighty Sir," and a moment later two beautiful damsels throw over his shoulders "a long mantle of fine scarlet." Not only this, but the courtyard is soon crowded with domestics who by the Duke's order, sent ahead, cry out: "Welcome, welcome, the Flower and Cream of Knight-Errantry!" "All which," says Cervantes, "agreeably surprised the Don, and this was indeed the first day he knew and firmly believed himself to be a real knight-errant, and that his knighthood was more than fancy; finding himself treated just as he had read the brothers of the order were entertained in former ages." We can have our own opinion as to this last, even though it is Cervantes who has spoken. If his tongue is not in his cheek, ours may be in ours, and for that matter the Don's in his, though certainly an immense hospitality still awaits him. There is, for instance, the first dinner, soon to be announced. Dressed in a magnificent cloak and cap—by Sancho, remember, and not by the mischievous maids assigned for the purpose—he enters a room of state where damsels and pages, arranged in rows, in turn conduct him to another room where a table is sumptuously set for him, the Duke, the Duchess, and a grave ecclesiastic who will have his own view of our hero.

The whole of this episode is a novel by itself, and needs to be read in order to be known in its full beauty. It has its own form and contains its own characters. The Duke, for instance, seems to be less malicious than his wife, though to be sure it is he who conceives the great hoax of the island where Sancho is sent to govern. Sancho had been about to desert his master when the Duchess came in sight. Don Quixote had promised him an island, and no island had appeared. Now by an irony it was within his reach at the very moment he contemplated his treason—or pretended to contemplate it, for it was impossible that he should ever leave Don Quixote's side. Well, Sancho will have his island, and will govern it so much better than the Duke supposes that the Duke in turn will be confounded. But throughout that first dinner and the evening which follows it the Duke is a gentleman of Don Quixote's own sort. When four damsels, bent upon a prank of their own, enter the dining room with water, towels, and soap, and lather the knight's beard so that he looks funny enough to kill them with laughter, though of course they do not laugh, the Duke orders them to give him the same treatment; they do so, and leave the room well paid for their frolic. They had exceeded their duty, and perhaps it occurs to the Duke that they have insulted the knight in a fashion not conformable to the tenor of the hoax. Also, there is the moment after dinner when the Duchess interrupts Don Quixote's panegyric on the theme of Dulcinea's beauty. He has been saying that only "Ciceronian and Demosthenian eloquence" could do justice to such beauty. "Pray, Sir," asks the Duchess, "what do you mean by that word Demosthenian?" Perhaps she thinks it a mad coinage, or a mere nonsense word spoken by an irresponsible person. "Demosthenian eloquence, Madam," says the Don, "is as much as to say, the eloquence of Demosthenes, and the Ciceronian that of Cicero, the two greatest orators that ever were in the world." " 'Tis true," says the Duke; "and you but showed your ignorance, my dear, in asking such a question."

The hoax turns out to be not only immense but multiple. There are hoaxes within hoaxes, as if the whole were a Chinese box for some philosopher's diversion. And that is true; and the philosopher is Cervantes. There is, for instance, the Disenchantment of Dulcinea, which ends with Sancho's paying Don Quixote for the way his leg had been pulled at the Cave of Montesinos. At first, however, it seems a triumph for the master. The Duchess, having wormed out of Sancho the story of the Cave, sees a chance to have fun by putting on an elaborate masque or pageant in the course of which it will be manifested by the powers of darkness that they are willing to free Dulcinea of her enchantment if Sancho will contract to give himself three thousand lashes. There will be no end to the story of these lashes, which if one likes are the Don's revenge for Sancho's intended deception of him at Toboso. Sancho, naturally, has no liking for them, and imposes conditions at the very start: none of them shall draw blood, and any of them that misses its mark may be counted just the same. But even then, and with the additional understanding that he can take as long as he pleases to complete the count, he delays and delays, so that the last lash is delivered long after he and his master have left the Duke. At one time he is so far behind that Don Quixote, who says he is impatient for Dulcinea to be free, offers to pay him to go faster. He will finally fool Don Quixote by retiring into a forest and whipping trees, groaning dismally the while.

Sancho gets even on the Wooden Horse, which he and Don Quixote must ride in connection with still another hoax that does not matter here. They ride the horse blindfolded, so as not to see the universe they travel through. The horse of course does not move, though bellows are blown to simulate a wind. When the adventure is over, nevertheless, Sancho has a confession to make. He had cheated; he had lifted his blindfold a little and looked out. And what had he seen? Oh, wonders! "I spied the earth a hugeous way afar off below me, heaven bless us, no bigger than a mustard seed; and the men walking to and fro upon it, not much larger than hazel nuts." The Duchess finds some failure of proportion here, but Sancho dismisses her objection and soars on. "I saw myself so near heaven that between the top of my cap and the main sky there was not a span and a half. And forsooth, what a hugeous place it is! And we happened to travel that road where the seven she-goatstars were; and faith and troth, I had such a mind to play with them, having once been a goatherd myself, that I fancy I'd have cried myself to death had I not done it. I sneaked down very soberly from behind my master, without telling any living soul, and played and leaped about for three quarters of an hour by the clock with the pretty nanny-goats, who are as sweet and fine as so many marigolds or gilly-flowers." Don Quixote has prepared his own tale of what he saw, but it cannot match this, and he takes refuge in the higher criticism. "It was impossible," he says, "for us to reach that part where are the Pleiades, or the Seven Goats as Sancho calls them, without being consumed in the elemental fire; and therefore Sancho either lies or dreams." When Sancho protests that it was no dream, Don Quixote has only one card left to play. "Sancho," he whispers a little later, "since thou wouldst have us believe what thou hast seen in heaven, I desire thee to believe what I saw in Montesino's cave. Not a word more." Nor is it necessary. The two men's legs are now of equal length.

When the great hoax is over and our heroes are at liberty to move on, they are happy in the same way that we are happy. For the jest has run its course and even become a little stale, just as the two noble hosts have dwindled in our estimation. Not only have they gone to absurd lengths to prove our hero mad; they have helped, without ever knowing it, to prove him sane. If nothing else, the remark whispered to Sancho makes it clear that Don Quixote knows where he is and what he is doing. He knows where he is, and he does not think it is heaven. Were he simply mad, he might suppose it was. But he is glad to get away from a part that has been both exhausting and humiliating to perform. The Duke and the Duchess, who took it for granted that he thought himself in heaven, had not made good their assumption by being equal in courtesy to him. He was acting and they were acting; but they did not know the part to its depth. He knew it as deep as the mind and the soul can go. There was no difference between his courtesy and the courtesy of any true knight you please. Theirs was but the exaggerated gesture of pretenders who feel themselves superior to the virtue they copy. Don Quixote, hailing liberty regained, rides back into the simpler world of earth where his imagination is at home. It had accommodated itself with skill to the hocus-pocus that surrounded him in a house whose inmates were dishonest. Now for the great world where honor and dishonor fight with each other every day.

3

The whole of *Don Quixote* is either a series of adventures or a series of conversations. More properly, since many of the conversations are about the adventures, before as well as after they take place, it is both series intertwined. The book, that is to say, is neither all action nor all talk. It is not a yarn, and it is not a philosophical dialogue. Its events are of deep interest to the intellect, and its discussions advance the plot. So it is dangerous to emphasize the one thing at the expense of the other, though more will be lost by ignoring the speeches than will be lost by overlooking the overt, the visible deeds. The deeds, in fact, are less likely to be overlooked than the commentaries upon them, and sometimes it appears that they are the only items a reader remembers: *Don Quixote*, by the common account, is nothing but a story of a foolish, fond old man who began by making a mistake about windmills and went on to make innumerable other mistakes of the same description.

But this is not what one finds if one reads the book with loving and continuous care. For then it turns out that the hero is quite as much a talking as a doing man. And the final memory may be of a voice, magnificent not merely for itself but for the mind that inspires it, which one will not expect to hear again in any book. The eloquence of Don Quixote is in a class by itself. No other hero ever talked as richly or as well. And this may seem strange if what he wanted to be, or to seem to be, was a knight at arms. The knights of the romances spoke handsomely upon occasion, but for the most part they rode and fought. If Palmerin of England, whom the barber and the curate ranked second to Amadis of Gaul, is an outstanding exception to this rule, he is also an outstanding bore. Don Quixote, who talks ten times as much, is anything you please but he is never a bore. He is busier talking about knights than being one; he contemplates rather than fulfills the role; but precisely there is where his charm comes in.

"A man that talks well," remarks the Duke, "can never talk

too much." He is speaking of Sancho, and he does not mean the compliment, though indeed he should; but any good reader will accept it for Sancho's master, whose resonant tones, matching so perfectly his resonant thoughts, make of the entire book a musical work distinguished for the depth and variety of its sound. The style of Don Quixote is perhaps the most delicious style in any literature. This man can say anything, short or long; he knows his way as genius does through the labyrinth of intellect and language; and there is endless learning at his command. He is never out of touch with his erudition, which certain of his interlocutors consider excessive but which all of them recognize as native to a mind both spacious and subtle, both full to overflowing and free to overflow. The slightest object can remind him of vast subjects for discourse: an acorn of the Golden Age, a millpond of the seven seas. And often he is wise. Men who see him coming and think him simply crazy remain in his path so that they may exchange words with him and extract amusement from the poor mad things he will say. But most of the things he says do not strike them as poor or mad, and they are puzzled. There is a soundness in his views that moves them almost to complain. Such a man has no right to be so interesting or so true. Of course he is false with respect to knighthood; he is clearly insane when it comes to that; yet of any other matter he has a gentleman's, a scholar's, understanding. He is acute and humane; and he evidently knows his Aristotle.

It never occurs to these men that because he is right about so many other things he may be right about knight-errantry too. Nor may it occur to us who have listened to him night and day since the book began. But the reason in our case is a little different. His wisdom has long since ceased to seem inconsistent with the rest of him, whatever the rest of him is. We have fallen so deeply in love with his manner that we have forgotten how to judge his matter; we have lost in large part our interest in the question of his madness. Would that all men could talk as he talks. He is king of his world, and he is perhaps the king of any world we can imagine. When we see him dressing for dinner, whether at the Duke's house or at the meanest inn, we know that he will descend to dominate a dinner table where others tolerantly await him. He will determine the topics to be discussed, and he will not only lead but ornament the discussion.

The topic he likes best is his beloved books of chivalry—*were* they true and *are* they true? And if they seem so real that we delight to read them, what is the meaning of our delight? Is it entertainment or instruction, is it belief or make-belief? He will pursue this theme with anybody: the barber and the curate, Don Vivaldo, the Canon of Toledo, Don Diego and his son, or the Duke's priest who is so sure that he himself is right. With the Canon of Toledo the discussion branches out until it takes in such subsidiary topics as the difference between poetry and history, and the difference too between learned and unlearned readers; for both have their claims, and the greatest writers condescend to neither. With Don Lorenzo, Don Diego's son, the talk is all of poetry, an art which the young man has practiced with but small success to date. He is encouraged by Don Quixote, whom he considers mad on every other subject, to believe himself a good poet; for the old stranger seems to know a great deal about the art, and who is to say whether he flatters or not the author of the specimens placed before him?

But there is no finer disquisition on the reality of knights than one which runs its course at the inn while Don Quixote sleeps. He takes no part in it, of course; and yet his very presence, snoring in another room, lifts the speakers to a height they would not otherwise attain. He is not only eloquent in himself, but the cause that eloquence is in other men—or as it chances now, in men and girls, for the innkeeper's daughter and Maritornes have their own testimony to give. The barber has proposed that the innkeeper's books of chivalry be burned as Don Quixote's were; though the curate votes that some of them be saved because they are true histories. Both critics mystify their host, who has never thought very much about either poetry or history. He is willing to believe whatever he sees in print; but mainly the books in question give him pleasure and keep him alive. And others, too. "In harvest-time, a great many of the reapers come to drink here in the heat of the day, and he that can read best among us takes up one of these books; and all the rest of us, sometimes thirty or more, sit round about him, and listen with such pleasure that we think neither of sorrow nor care; as for my own part, when I hear the mighty blows and dreadful battles of these knights-errant, I have half a mind to be one myself, and am raised to such a life and briskness that I frighten away old age; I could sit and hear them from morning till night." He is in truth another Don Quixote, though he will never take to the road. If he did, observes his wife, he might lose some of the ill humor that makes him hard to live with. His daughter confesses that it is not so much the fighting as the love that interests her. And yet it is a painful interest, since so much of the love is what you could call unhappy. "Indeed the sad lamentations of the poor knights, for the loss of their mistresses, sometimes makes me cry like anything. . . . I will never give anybody reason to call me tigress and lioness, and I don't know how many other ugly names, as those ladies are often called, and I think they deserve yet worse, so they do; for they can neither have soul nor conscience to let such fine gentlemen die or run mad for a sight of them. What signifies all their fiddling and coyness? If they are civil women, why don't they marry 'em, for that's all their knights would be at?" Her father, however, brings the conversation back to the prowess, true or false, of such heroes as Cirongilio of Thrace, "who, as you may read there, going by water one day, was assaulted by a fiery serpent in the middle of the river; he presently leaped nimbly upon her back, and hanging by her scaly neck, grasped her throat fast with both his arms, so that the serpent, finding herself almost strangled, was forced to dive into the water to save herself, and carried the knight, who would not quit his hold, to the very bottom, where he found a stately palace, and such stately gardens that 'twas a wonder; and straight the serpent turned into a very old man, and told him such things as were never heard nor spoken." Here, hundreds of pages before the Don descends into its depths, is the Cave of Montesinos. But the Don is sound asleep and must have that adventure by himself.

He has it, rather, with Sancho. And with Sancho he has the most as well as the best of his conversations. Perhaps he had not expected this when he picked his fat little neighbor to go along with him as squire. He could think as he pleased about the horse he would call his steed and the rustic maiden he would apostrophize as his lady, just as he could pretend without difficulty that the armor he wore was brilliant and new. None of those could speak up and refute him. But now this squire would talk. And what would he say? Certainly he did not look and could not be made to look like the fair young fellows who went forth with Amadis and their kind, dreaming appropriate dreams of the day when they themselves would kneel before a king and be received into the order they adored; dreaming too in their delicate hearts of slender princesses whose names they were ambitious to carry about the world on loving lips. Sancho was not like that, nor was the peasant woman he had married. Doubtless he would be a failure when it came to words; the problem would be to keep him silent; or if not that, to educate him in the rudiments of his role. For he would have to know that he played a part in the same way, though not with the same success, that his master did. The only question was, could he be induced to learn it? Could he become serious about it, as good actors do about their lines? The innkeeper who had knighted Don Quixote was no longer present to embarrass him. He was not a king, but one could say he was and not be contradicted. Sancho might confound his lord at every turn; he might keep on being himself. And that, as we all know, is exactly what Sancho did. And that, as we know too, is why his master loved him in the end. But there were moments of panic before this end was reached. Sancho was always a burden and a care. He had perpetually to be reminded and instructed. And much of the conversation between the two has that for its purpose. Nor do we always notice that Don Quixote's talk concerns the role that Sancho plays rather than some delusion that they are respectively knight and squire. The Don never assumes that Sancho does not know who his master is. He knows he knows it as well as he knows the name of Dapple. There is no pretense between the two, no mutual deception. Or if there is, they both have fun with the fact. And the fun they have is the clearest proof that Sancho is not stupid nor the Don insane.

An early example is their discourse concerning food. They have just left the Biscayan who, though vanquished, had cut away half of Don Quixote's ear; and the knight is both hurt and hungry. "At this time," he says, "I'd have thee see whether thou hast anything to eat in thy wallet, that we may afterward seek for some castle where we may lodge this night and make the balsam I told thee; for I protest my ear smarts extremely." "I have here an onion," replies Sancho, "a piece of cheese, and a few stale crusts of bread; but sure such coarse fare is not for such a brave knight as your worship." "Thou art grossly mistaken, friend Sancho. Know, that 'tis the glory of knights-errant to be whole months without eating; and when they do, they fall upon the first thing they meet with, though it be never so homely. Hadst thou but read as many books as I have done, thou hadst been better informed as to that point; for though I think I have read as many histories of chivalry in my time as any other man, I never could find that the knights-errant ever ate, unless it was by mere accident, or when they were invited to great feasts or royal banquets; at other times they indulged themselves with little other food besides their thoughts. Though it is not to be imagined they could live without supplying the exigencies of human nature, as being after all no more than mortal men, yet 'tis likewise to be supposed, that as they spent the greatest part of their lives in forests and deserts, and always destitute of a cook, consequently their usual food was but such coarse country fare as thou now offerest me. Never then make thyself uneasy about what pleases me, friend Sancho, nor pretend to make a new world, nor to unhinge the very constitution and ancient customs of knight-errantry." "I beg your worship's pardon; for as I was never bred a scholar, I may chance to have missed in some main point of your laws of knighthood; but from this time forward I'll be sure to stock my wallet with all sorts of dry fruits for you, because your worship's a knight; as for myself, who am none, I'll provide poultry and other substantial victuals." "I don't say, Sancho, that a knight-errant is obliged to feed altogether upon fruit; I only mean, that this was their common food, together with some roots and herbs which they found up and down the fields, of all which they had a perfect knowledge, as I myself have." " 'Tis a good thing," agrees Sancho, "to know those herbs; for I am much mistaken, or that kind of knowledge will stand us in good stead ere long. In the meantime here's what good Heaven has sent us." And they fall to heartily together.

Nor is the subject finished there, for soon they join some goatherds at their evening meal and the question arises as to whether the two of them shall eat together in the company of others. The Don is certain that they should. " 'Tis my pleasure," he insists, "that thou sit thee down by me, in the company of these good people; and that there be no difference now observed between thee and me, thy natural lord and master; that thou eat in the same dish and drink in the same cup; for it may be said of knight-errantry, as of love, that it makes all things equal." "I thank your worship, but to deal plainly and truly with you, I had rather munch a crust of brown bread and an onion in a corner, without any more ado or ceremony, then feed upon turkey at another man's table, where one is fain to sit mincing and chewing his meat an hour together, drink little, be always wiping his fingers and his chops, and never dare to cough nor sneeze, though he had never so much a mind to it, nor do a many things which a body may do freely by one's self. Therefore, good Sir, change those tokens of your kindness, which I have a right to by being your worship's squire, into something that may do me more good. As for these honors, I heartily thank you as much as if I had accepted 'em, but yet I give up my right to 'em from this time to the world's end." "Talk no more," replies Don Quixote, "but sit thee down, for the humble shall be exalted." So Sancho loses that argument, just as he loses many an argument on the sister subject, sleep. "Sleep, Sancho, for thou wert born to sleep." And Sancho, willingly confuted, sleeps; while his master, who might not mind a wink himself, sits or paces and composes madrigals which he has proved to be more precious than the sweet closing of eyelids even when one is tired almost to death.

"Talk no more, for the humble shall be exalted." The time comes, however, when Sancho is sentenced to silence for the opposite reason. The abortive adventure with the fulling-mills is under discussion as every adventure will henceforth be; and Sancho has mocked his master's bravery of the night before—mocked it so merrily that the Don has struck him. "I did but joke a little," says Sancho, rubbing his shoulders and asking pardon. It is then the knight's turn to be magnanimous; yet he has one further thing to say. "Sancho, I prithee think no more of my severity; thou knowest a man cannot always command the first impulse of his passions. On the other side, let me advise thee not to be so saucy for the future, and not to assume that strange familiarity with me which is so unbecoming in a servant. I protest, in such a vast number of books of knighthood as I have read, I never found that any squire was ever allowed so great a freedom of speech with his master as thou takest with me; and truly I look upon it to be a great fault in us both; in thee for disrespecting me, and in me for not making myself more respected. Gandalin, Amadis of Gaul's squire, though he was earl of the Firm Island, yet never spoke to his master but with cap in hand, his head bowed, and his body half bent, after the Turkish manner. But what shall we say of Gasabal, Don Galaor's squire, who was such a strict observer of silence that, to the honor of his marvelous taciturnity, he gave the author occasion to mention his name but once in that voluminous authentic history? From all this, Sancho, I would have thee make this observation, that there ought to be a distance kept between the master and the man, the knight and the squire. Therefore, once more I tell thee, let's live together for the future more according to the due decorum of our respective degrees, without giving one another any further vexation on this account; for after all, 'twill always be the worse for you on whatsoever occasion we happen to disagree." "You may be sure," says Sancho after a while, "I'll not so much as offer to open my lips to jibe or joke at your doings, but always stand in awe of you, and honor you as my lord and master." "By doing so," replies the Don, "thy days shall be long on the face of the earth; for next to our parents we ought to respect our masters, as if they were our fathers."

They ride on, and Sancho never speaks unless he is spoken to—never, that is, until the middle of the morning, when he suddenly says: "Pray, Sir, will you give me leave to talk to you a little? For since you have laid that bitter command upon me, to hold my tongue, I've had four or five quaint conceits that have rotted in my gizzard, and now I've another at my tongue's end that I would not for anything should miscarry." "Say it!" cries Don Quixote; "but be short, for no discourse can please when too long." The discourse concerns the disadvantages to them both of the obscurity in which they travel; nobody knows what they are doing, no author is taking notes that might blossom into a romance. Perhaps they should go and serve some emperor or prince who has minstrels and scribes at his command. Don Quixote, alert to this cue, indulges in marvelous daydreams of such a consummation to his career; he anticipates, in fact, the reception they will have at the Duke's house in Part II. But at this moment he must be glad that Sancho has broken the silence imposed upon him. He had never meant it anyway, or expected that Sancho would do as he was told. For even so soon his fat companion has shown himself to be a wonder among the talkers of the world. The Don has infinite resources within himself; yet how much better it is to have one by his side whose every remark, however ignorant it may be, is stimulating to the brain and tongue. But he maintains the fiction a little longer, if only that he may relish the truth more.

The end of the experiment comes as the two of them ride into the Black Mountain. "Thus they traveled for a while," Cervantes tells us, "without speaking a word to each other. Sancho, almost dead, and ready to burst for want of a little chat, waited with great impatience to begin, not daring to speak first, since his strict injunction of silence. But at last, not being able to keep his word any longer: 'Good your worship,' quoth he, 'give me your blessing and leave to be gone, I beseech you, that I may go home to my wife and children, where I may talk till I am weary, and nobody can hinder me; for I must needs tell you, that for you to think to lead me a jaunt through hedge and ditch, over hills and dales, by night and by day, without daring to open my lips, is to bury me alive. Could beasts speak, as they did in Aesop's time, 'twould not have been half so bad with me; for then might I have communed with my ass as I pleased, and have forgot my ill fortune. But to trot on in this fashion, all the days of my life, after adventures, and to light on nothing but thumps, kicks, cuffs, and be tossed in a blanket, and after all, forsooth, to have a man's mouth sewed up, without daring to speak one's mind, I say it again, no living soul can endure it.' 'I understand thee, Sancho,' answered Don Quixote, 'thou lingerest with impatience to exercise thy talking faculty. Well, I am willing to free thy tongue from this restraint that so cruelly pains thee, upon condition that the time of this license shall not extend beyond that of our continuance in these mountains.' "

But we hear no more of the condition. Don Quixote never muzzles his best friend again. They will have quarrels, and Sancho will be reminded that he is insolent beyond endurance, and illiterate to boot; but his master does not repeat the mistake he knows he has made. Nor is Sancho unaware that he knows it. The two of them have been fencing for position, and here now the position is: They will talk to the end of the world, on every subject under the sun, and it will never be true that one of them enjoys it less than the other.

Sancho's enjoyment is such that when he strikes for wages at the beginning of Part II he cannot strike to the bitter end: the losing of his job. Don Quixote, preparing for his third sally from home, seems to know this very well; and to know, furthermore, how Sancho can be brought around. Carrasco has offered to be squire, and Sancho has heard the offer. "Well, Sancho," says his employer, "did not I tell thee I should not want squires? Behold who offers me his service, the most excellent bachelor of arts Sampson Carrasco, the perpetual darling of the Muses and glory of the Salamanca schools, sound and active of body, patient of labor, inured to abstinence, silent in misfortune, and in short, endowed with all the accomplishments that constitute a squire. But forbid it, Heaven, that to indulge my private inclinations I should presume to weaken the whole body of learning by removing from it so substantial a pillar, so vast a repository of sciences, and so eminent a branch of the liberal arts. No, my friend, remain thou another Sampson in thy country, be the honor of Spain, and the delight of thy ancient parents; I shall content myself with any squire, since Sancho does not vouchsafe to go with me." "I do, I do, I do vouchsafe!" cries Sancho, with tears in his eyes. Of course he vouchsafes. Where else would he hear a voice like that, saying such absurd, such sublime, such beautiful things? He will live with that voice till it finds its own silence, as to his grief and ours eventually it does.

So the conversation of this pair flows on. And one sign of its excellence is that each listens to and learns from the other. Don Quixote, for example, learns how to respect proverbs. He began by despising Sancho's addiction to the vulgar vice of letting others say for him what he should say himself. A proverb has been defined as the wisdom of many and the wit of one; but the one is long since dead, and we are his slaves if we can do no better than take what he has tossed us out of old time. The Don is too proud of his own rhetoric to exchange it for that of some country wit whose lineage he does not know. What he gradually realizes is that Sancho's scholarship in the field of proverbs is immense. The little man knows millions of them; they dribble from him, they pop out of him like peas out of a pod, they pepper his entire discourse until it is in fact too highly seasoned—the wood of his subject is lost among the multitude of waving trees. Sancho is a true son of Spain, a country notoriously rich in popular sayings; but the thing has become in him, says his master, worse even than a vice. It is a disease, a sickness of the mind. Yet Don Quixote feels the fascination too, and at last he is infected. He begins to match the apothegms of Sancho with dozens of his own. He will never catch up with the virtuoso at his side; he has read too many books for that, and been lost in too many abstractions. Still, he does his best; and Sancho is much pleased.

And soon enough the servant shows that some at least of his master's style has rubbed off on him. They are riding away from those strolling players whom Don Quixote has extolled as the looking-glasses of human life. "Prithee tell me," he continues, "hast thou never seen a play acted, where kings, emperors, prelates, knights, ladies, and other characters are introduced on the stage? One acts a ruffian, another a soldier;

this man a cheat, and that a merchant; one plays a designing fool, and another a foolish lover; but the play done, and the actors undressed, they are all equal, and as they were before. Just such a comedy is acted on the great stage of the world, where some play the emperors, others the prelates, and in short, all the parts that can be brought into a dramatic piece; till death, which is the catastrophe and end of the action, strips the actors of all their marks of distinction, and levels their quality in the grave." "A rare comparison," says Sancho, "but not so new but that I have heard it over and over. Just such another is that of a game at chess, where while the play lasts, every piece has its particular office; but when the game's over, they are all mingled and huddled together, and clapped into a bag, just as when life's ended we are laid up in the grave." To which Don Quixote, nobly overlooking the palpable hit at his cliché, returns a handsome compliment. "Truly, Sancho, thy simplicity lessens, and thy sense improves every day." "And good reason why," says Sancho, who is not to be outdone in courtesy. "Some of your worship's wit must needs stick to me; for your dry unkindly land, with good dunging and tilling, will in time yield a good crop. I mean, Sir, that the dung and muck of your conversation being thrown on the barren ground of my wit, together with the time I have served your worship and kept you company; which is, as a body may say, the tillage; I must needs bring forth blessed fruit at last, so as not to shame my master, but keep in the paths of good manners, which you have beaten into my sodden understanding."

The compliment is not without its jest, but so of all compliments that equals pay each other. The knight and the squire are well on their way to an equality more warm and living than that of undressed actors or that of chessmen clapped into a bag; or even that of masters and servants who eat at the same table. They are finally, as it were, one flesh. And if Don Quixote, granting this, says that he is the head and Sancho the body, that is only his way of keeping decorum. He would never deny what Sancho says to the Duke's clergyman: "I have stuck close to my good master, and kept him company this month; and now he and I are all one, and I must be as he is, if it be Heaven's blessed will." He might not like so well the beginning of a similar speech made to the Duchess, but he would clap at the conclusion. "I am a fool, that's certain," confides Sancho to that noble lady, "for if I'd been wise I had left my master many a fair day since. But I must follow him through thick and thin. I have eaten his bread, I love him well, and nothing but death can part us." When Don Quixote trembles and blushes at the Duke's table because Sancho is talking out of turn, and talking as always much too long, it is as if he felt a portion of his own wit to have gone astray. The brother has escaped the keeper, though of course he can be brought back.

Equality in these men has reached that height which only the greatest comedy exposes. Don Quixote had been right when he particularly praised comedians and comedies for their power to give "a just idea of Nature." If it be true that only God can understand how men are equal, then comedy deserves all praise for its attempt to be divine. The human comedy God writes would seem to be the thing great artists copy. Cervantes copies it in every page of his all but inhumanly charitable book. In that book even Rozinante and Dapple, the noble horse and the lowly ass, are lost without each other. And Sancho is as close to Dapple as he is to the Don. Losing him once and finding him again, he runs to embrace him and kiss him, and call him his darling and treasure, the delight of his eyes, his dearest companion, "as if," says Cervantes, "the beast had been a rational creature." The beast, Cervantes goes on to say, accepts the kisses without a word. No matter, though. Don Quixote will have words, and words to waste.

His words of instruction as Sancho goes off to govern his "island"—a dry little town with walls and a thousand inhabitants, a dependency of the Duke which his steward has rehearsed in its part—are doubtless all wasted. They are out of Aristotle, Plato, and one does not know how many other political philosophers; and they are wise words of course; but Sancho does not need them. Don Quixote supposed he did, and hence a lecture that went even so far as to caution the new dignitary against excesses of eating and sleeping, either excess being as bad for the brain as a plethora of proverbs. The two men part with tears, since by this time they have really become inseparable, and Sancho proceeds to astonish everybody by his wisdom. It is the wisdom of Solomon rather than of Aristotle, as three cases brought before him prove even to those who stand about in the expectation that he will make a fool of himself. The tailor and his five caps, the debtor and his cane, and the powerful doxy whom Sancho maneuvers into showing a strength she should have used in defense of the virtue she pretends she has lost by force—the truth about no one of these is missed by a man who, however, deficient his academic education, is a perfect judge of character. Sancho's knowledge of others begins, one may think, in the knowledge he has of himself. It is a plainer brand of self-knowledge than manifests itself in his master, who indeed has more to know, since of the two he is the more complicated person. Sancho, to be sure, does not see through the fiction of a court physician who in the guise of one who would watch his diet starves him almost to death. He complains of this in one of his charming letters to the Don, who meanwhile is having troubles of his own in the madhouse of the Duke, and who reports them too in loving letters which the governor is delighted to receive; the separated friends cannot after all break off communication with each other. But Sancho is on the whole as surprising to those who watch him conduct affairs as Don Quixote ever was to those who heard him conduct conversations.

The same mistake is made about both men: one cannot be wise because he is mad, and the other must be a fool because he is illiterate. So far as the reader is concerned, there is no sweeter evidence of Sancho's sanity, not to say his maturity, than is provided in the speech he makes to the young brother and sister whom the town watchmen bring before him as he makes his nightly rounds. What started as a prank has ended in arrest. But Sancho has straightened things out, and how he speaks: "Truly, gentlefolks, here's a little piece of childish folly; and to give an account of this wild frolic, and slip of youth, there needed not all these sighs and tears, nor these hems and haws and long excuses. Could not you, without any more ado, have said, our names are so and so, and we stole out of our father's house for an hour or two, only to ramble about the town and satisfy a little curiosity, and there had been an end of the story, without all this weeping and wailing." "You say very well," the damsel protests, "but you may imagine that in the trouble and fright I was in, I could not behave myself as I should have done." "Well," says Sancho, "there's no harm done; go along with us, and we'll see you home to your father's; perhaps you mayn't yet be missed. But have a care how you gad abroad to see fashions another time. Don't be too venturesome. An honest maid should be still at home, as if she had one leg broken. A hen and a woman are lost by rambling; and she that longs to see, longs also to be seen. I need say no more."

And now for the sequel as Cervantes tells it. "The young gentleman thanked the Governor for his civility, and then went home under his conduct. Being come to the house, the young spark threw a little stone against one of the iron-barred windows; and presently a maidservant, who sat up for them, came down, opened the door, and let him and his sister in. The Governor with his company then continued his rounds, talking all the way they went of the genteel carriage and beauty of the brother and sister, and the great desire these poor children had to see the world by night."

Sancho in the end resigns as governor and rejoins his master—falling first, however, into a pit out of which Don Quixote has to pull him as he himself had been pulled up out of the Cave of Montesinos—and soon enough the two great friends leave the castle of the Duke behind them, bent on further adventures. But the further adventures are all downhill. Their enthusiasm is somehow spent, as in a sense the vigor of Cervantes is. Some of the best and deepest things are still to happen; the narrative means most at its very end; yet so far as the spirits of the heroes are concerned there can be no true recovery from the hell of hoax through which both men have passed.

And if a kind of quiet has descended upon the heart of Don Quixote, so that he is free to meditate upon a simpler role that he might play, the role of shepherd which we know has always competed in his mind with that of knight, Cervantes does not permit him to enjoy this quiet. Twice he dreams the pastoral dream, and twice—upon the instant, too, of his indulgence—peace for him is shattered. The great musician who constructs the work twice introduces the new theme, but each time murders it with thunder, with a burst of kettledrums. Don Quixote, stumbling upon some youths and maidens who have dressed as shepherds so that they may call themselves Arcadians, is inspired to make a suitable speech in honor of the beauty of the girls; and then here comes a herd of bulls to ride him down. It is a terrible humiliation, painful to both his body and his mind; but it will be matched by another one not too many pages on, when, musing with Sancho on the pastoral existence they may sometime lead together—he gets so far as to imagine the names they will take, Quixotis in his case, Pansino in Sancho's, though Sancho rather favors Teresona as a tribute to his wife—here comes a herd of boars to ride him down again. And if with his last breath he is tempted a third time to consider the role of amorous shepherd, the punishment is then as final as it is swift; he dies, and never dreams again.

The time comes, in other words, when Don Quixote decides to stop acting altogether. The role of knight has never pleased; and heaven itself would seem to be saying that the pastoral part is not so much as to be imagined. There is nothing to do but to go home where some have said he should have stayed in the first place. He can scarcely agree with this, nor can we agree who would never have known him had he obeyed his niece; yet he does go, and the story is soon over. He goes, for one thing, because he must keep his word. Carrasco has caught up with him again, and this time he makes sure that when they ride against each other it will be Don Quixote who is unhorsed. That happens, and then Don Quixote is obliged to remember the condition he accepted: if defeated, to return to his village and live peaceably there for the whole of one year. He remembers, and he consents. It never occurs to him to do otherwise, nor has Carrasco doubted that he would keep his word. A madman might have forgotten ever giving such a word; a maniac would almost certainly demolish it now. But Don Quixote turns the head of Rozinante home—sadly, to be sure, yet resolutely. His last act as a knight is possibly his truest. He is faithful to his vow.

At home in bed, for he is very tired, he shows no disposition to discuss either knights or shepherds further. He announces to his niece that he is dying, and asks her to bring the barber, the curate, and Carrasco so that they may hear his recantation. They are coming anyway, for they are concerned about their friend. But their concern grows into consternation when they hear what he has to say. He has never seemed madder than he does now. "My good friends," he says, "I have happy news to tell you. I am no longer Don Quixote de La Mancha. . . . I declare myself an enemy to Amadis of Gaul and his whole generation; all profane stories of knight-errantry, all romances I detest. I have a true sense of the danger of reading them, and of all my past follies, and through Heaven's mercy, and my own experience, I abhor them." This sounds to the three men standing at his bedside so much like a new frenzy of some sort that their instinct is to humor him in it as drunkards are placated with more drink. Carrasco says he has heard that Dulcinea is at last disenchanted. To which her one-time lover supplies an answer as soft as it is decisive, as sweet as it is bitter. "No more of that, I beseech you. Pray, gentlemen, let us be serious. I want a priest to receive my confession, and a scrivener to draw up my will. There is no trifling at a time like this. I must take care of my soul."

It is like the answer given to Sancho when he rushes in a few minutes later and accuses his master of the extreme folly: he plans to die while he is still alive. Sancho, weeping between his brave words, does all that eloquence can do to recommend the shepherd's life they have thought of living, and to explain away the recent disaster in the field that has brought his master home; it was his fault, he suggests, for not having tightened Rozinante's girth; and anyway it was but one of many misfortunes that a true knight must expect. "Soft and fair," cuts in the voice of Don Quixote. "Never look for birds of this year in the nests of the last." Properly for the friend addressed, it is a proverb: the last that either one of them will deliver. And the gentleman who speaks it does not stay for an answer. Out of the book and out of the world he goes.

What had he been in the book, and what is he now in the world? In the world he is as many things as there are theories about him; and in the book too, no matter how carefully it is read, he may appear to be many men, or if he is one man, to have many minds and motives. His reality makes him indeed one man; there is none other like him in the world; but that same reality makes it impossible to know his thoughts.

Had he merely been seeking diversion: a bored old man with nothing to do? If so, he had had his diversion; choosing late in life, as Achilles had chosen in his youth, a life of glory over a life of peace and quiet, he had even had the glory; his life, such as it was, had come to an exciting end. This on the theory that he had been playing games; but they amused him no longer, so that now he could say, "let us be serious."

Had it all, on the other hand, been more than a diversion? Had he really believed in the utility of acting like a knight? The utility, and more than that, the duty in these degenerate times? And had it been borne in upon him at last that nobody cared how well he played such a part, or whether he played it at all? There seemed to be no audience; or if one collected, it was the opposite of sympathetic; it assisted him only in scorn; it hoaxed rather than upheld him, and he was weary of the hoax—of pretending he did not know it for what it was. The world refused to be entertained, or the earth edified; it remained just what it was, with him alone in it and quite absurd, a strolling player whom no one paid admission to see.

Or worse yet, what if he had fallen victim to his part? What if it had got into his blood and infected his brain? Not, surely, to the point of his thinking he was someone other than he was; but, just as bad, to the point of his believing that heaven could be built on earth, that ideas could take on physical form and have careers of flesh and blood—and cease, therefore, to be ideal. For a man of his faith, that would be no better than blasphemy; which may be why he at last rejected the romances as "profane," and why he addressed himself to the business of his soul. The soul does not put on armor, ride horses, and strike innocent people down. It contemplates perfection in the silence of eternity; it does not do, but be.

By the time Cervantes was finished with his book he was willing, no doubt, that we should think any or all of these things about its hero. And what shall he think about its author, what shall we assume his understanding was? It is likely that his own thought developed as he wrote, though we cannot see this happening, and it may be that his idea was simple and complete from the beginning. But what was his idea? If we say it was one that absorbs all of the ironies we find in *Don Quixote*, the very statement sounds absurd because it sounds so serious. Cervantes never seems to be serious. He is funny, he is superficial, he is queer, like life itself; but he never writes with the long face his critics put on. His hero is the loneliest man in literature, and the most abused; but Cervantes does not seem to want to save him. He lets every criticism be leveled at him, every epithet be heaped upon his head, without growing sentimental in his defense. We may grow sentimental about the Knight of the Woeful Figure, but we are not made of iron, of comedy's iron, as Cervantes was. The stuff of the book must have been the stuff of his very heart—which he did not wear on his sleeve.

We may conclude, and most of us do, that Don Quixote is the most perfect knight that ever lived; the only one, in fact, we can believe; but Cervantes never asks us to arrive at that conclusion. We may insist that instead of destroying the literature of knight-errantry Cervantes saved it by producing the one treatment of the subject that can be read forever; and that he did this by permitting his satire to ripen into comedy, his ridicule to deepen into love; yet over the centuries we still see his smile, and we can wonder how much of it is pity for us because we cannot leave his book alone. We may say that we honor and adore no man in literature or in life more than we honor and adore the stately friend of Sancho Panza. Cervantes, however, gives him no such honor; and, at least in our hearing, no such adoration. He merely gives him life. Perhaps it is the life that we should honor, looking at it plainly and looking then at one another; and grinning as we do.

# The Artist and the Changing World

IN TIMES like these the artist thinks of the world. He also thinks of himself; but the world changes faster than he does, and his eye cannot but follow it as far into the future as thought will go. Perhaps the activity should have been chronic with him; perhaps he should not be startled now. The world was always changing; it always will be changing; and who should know this better than the artist? He has to know, too, that the world never changes—the same old place, for better or for worse, simply looks different to its successive inhabitants. It is indeed different, and yet the *it* remains. The work of any artist, when it means enough to matter, means exactly this; and if it is given to few artists to mean so much, it is likewise given to few men to understand the mysteries of permanence and change. Few men of any sort have understood them, and no man has done so perfectly. The problem of the artist, like that of the philosopher, is immemorial and difficult and strange.

Just now the artist is particularly tempted to grow melancholy, forced as by many circumstances he is to remember how much art in the past has died. Whole languages and literatures have disappeared without even an echo to tell us how they sounded or what they said. Millenniums of plastic art have faded out of view, been buried under dust and clay, or crumbled to impalpable powder. And these are but the changes wrought by time's catastrophes, which in spite of many a poet's boast have silenced powerful rhyme as well as leveled marble and the gilded monuments of princes. The artist of today remembers other catastrophes, historical and human. He remembers that fashions change, that populations desert their teachers and audiences their entertainers. The spirit of an age, the character of a culture, demanded this or that; but then it ceased to do so and demanded something else. What had seemed determined was indeed determined, and not to be denied; yet all the while upheavals were preparing—the shores of taste were sinking, or were rising, and the artist who stood securely on them was getting ready, whether he knew it or not, to be submerged or beached; either to go down out of sight and be forgotten, or else to be left high and dry like any other unintelligible, irrelevant thing which only history can explain.

We like to believe that certain artists have been good enough —have been sufficient masters of permanence and change—to save themselves through all of time to come from dangers such as these. It is natural, for instance, to think of Shakespeare, who still outtops our knowledge and seems more fresh with every century he lives. He, if anybody, might be invincible to time and fashion. Yet Tolstoy, one of his great rivals for the privilege of surviving, has doubted that he is. And at this moment we are forced as seldom before to wonder what it would mean to have no such doubt at all. How much knowledge would we need? And knowledge of what things?

We know one thing already: that most of the books in our libraries, like many of the objects in our museums, have long since been dead. And their lifetimes were short. Admittedly a few were not so short; and here is Shakespeare, not to speak of Homer and the Bible, in all but innumerable editions which themselves suggest that no end is in sight. Yet something asks us now to be quite serious in our thought of this. Time ticks loudly in our ears, and change is real. Human history as we know it is still a recent thing. Say ten more thousand years pass; say a hundred thousand pass; say a million. Our imagination grows geological, grows astronomical, and staggers us. How can we know what things, if any, will last as long as we like to think society will last? There is even the fear that it and the earth are not to last; but forgetting this, again how can we know that changes are not coming which will doom our dearest monuments to extinction—the extinction of oblivion rather than of disappearance, of unintelligibility rather than of death by moisture and dry rot?

In times like these the artist thinks of this. But his talk is of his freedom—his freedom to survive, or else his freedom to go on doing what society has so far tolerated from his hand. The freedom of an artist, like the freedom of any individual, is what he thinks most personally about, since it feels to him like his very life. Yet it is not a simple thing, for all it may seem to be so in the minds of those who say it is only doing what one pleases. The trouble is, time also does what it pleases. Fashion, from which there is no appeal, does what it pleases. Thought marches on; society grows deaf and blind to what once entertained it; history is heartless, and leaves whole armies of artists stranded where they were. They were not free from that, however free each one of them was in his own private fancy. And it is worth remembering in how few ages of the world the artist's fancy has ever told him he was free. Liberty as you and I know it has been limited to a few brief periods of time and a few small areas of earth. We may take it for granted, but history does not.

To us it is a very precious thing, and not merely for the reason that it is the base of our operation as artists. It is no less precious, we assume, to the society of which we are a part; society, we have been taught to say, benefits in proportion as we are free to give it our vision without dictation or interference; society may not like what we do, but it would like still less what it thinks we ought to do; time will tell that we were right. We may not be free from the catastrophes that crush cities and bury civilizations under tidal water and volcanic ash; nor are we exempt from the law that inferior work dies of its own weakness; but our habit is to insist that nothing shall stand in the way of individual inspiration. The only penalty, if this inspiration be wrong or shallow, is the deserved penalty of failure; but meanwhile we shall not have been prevented from trying. The freedom of the artist is like the freedom of the citizen; he too must be left free to say in public what he thinks is true; suppress this right, and society suffers; suppress it long enough, and civilization dies.

For confirmation of this faith we point to the dead civilizations that archaeology has unburied. They were perfect of their kind, but the kind was doomed. The perfection was insect, not human—the right kind only if men were other than what they are, namely creatures who live longest together in happiness and strength when they hold on to the doctrine that every individual is somehow king; or rather, that he is both king and subject, with the duty to think and speak as he deems best; for only then will the structure of his community maintain that flexibility and inner well-being which guarantees survival. Archaeologists tell us that the dead cultures of Mesopotamia, Egypt, and Central America were too strictly ordered under priests and kings; that they were bureaucracies of vast refinement which nevertheless broke down when danger came; and that their artists were drones of the hive who likewise died in swarms and now have become, as indeed they always were, indistinguishable from one another. Our own civilization, that of Greece and Rome and modern Europe and America, still flourishes because it has kept the power to criticize and renew itself. It has changed again and again, but it has never become unrecognizable, and with every alteration it has taken on more life. And this is because its artists, like all of its citizens in whatever category, have remained free men. Such a civilization lives dangerously, and reaps glorious rewards.

But even our own history has periods when faith departed, or at least had to be re-examined. Plato's great dialogue of the *Republic* marks such a moment in the career of Athens. Change had reared its head, and war was shaking the foundations that men had supposed to be indestructible. How free could society afford to keep on being at a time when strains were felt in every portion of its superstructure? The *Republic* endeavored among other things to imagine the greatest change of all—one that would prevent change forever, and still leave Athens free from stagnation and Mesopotamian death. Socrates invited his friends to consider how they would proceed to build a state if they had the power and the opportunity to do so, and if they understood that they alone were responsible for its continuing health—really responsible, as no man born into an existing state ever is. Would they, for instance, be indifferent to its art? Would they have art at all; and if they did, would they make no attempt to censor and control it? What if it is true that bad art can enervate and corrupt a people? And if it is true, what should be done about it by such hypothetical authorities as Socrates conceived? The questions are famous, for they push the problem to its conclusion, and so we have never forgotten the *Republic*. We remember it most clearly in times of crisis like our own, when wars and dangers threaten. Meanwhile, we know, the wars of Greece went on and its civilization prepared to die; though it died only in that place, for it lived again, and it still lives in us.

And now we are having to decide again how free we can afford to be as artists and as men. Society has grown nervous. Real or imagined dangers revive the problem Plato saw. The twentieth century is different from the century before, and now in the very middle of it we wonder what is happening. Perhaps no man knows what is happening, or could possibly know; but every day we ask the question, and most days we are apprehensive. For something may be disappearing that we have always taken for granted. We may hope that it is not, but how can we be sure?

What every artist notices is that he lives in a society every member of which has a greater stake than formerly was the case in what we have come to call security. The world is a vast web that twitches incessantly with premonitions of disorder. Demagogues may exaggerate, and predatory persons may tell plain lies for their own advantage; but the people themselves are less carefree than once they were, and less certain, it would seem, that they will lose nothing by indulging the speculations of artists and philosophers. We accuse enemy countries of having murdered freedom, yet borrow from them some of their techniques; or if not that, we permit them to infect us with their doubt. We are not so sure but that some huge danger does after all exist, and that until the sky is clear we had better shut all doors against the storm. And nobody knows whose fault it is that this is so. Something has happened that no individual or party caused. We live with bureaucracy that turns in upon itself and contemplates its own elaboration, its own refinements which recall the delicate balances of those insect cultures long ago.

Public works have become more important than private houses. Education is moving toward the moment when all schools and universities will be administered by the state. Education will be too expensive for individuals to support; or else the state will doubt that individuals should do so. These may be the same thing in the end. The economic symptom is itself, perhaps, a symptom of something else. A thing becomes expensive when we have decided that we cannot afford it; the decision lies far back in our souls, or in the soul of society if society can be said to have one. We seem to think it does. We tax ourselves in the interest of a whole that is more precious than any of its parts. Even if it is not yet a monster, it estimates itself at the expense of individuals. It is the thing that must survive, and it acts as if it thought no man or artist could help it very much. It has its own laws and exacts its own penalties, the chief of which bear such cheerful names as obsolescence and liquidation.

The artist has all of this to think about today. He lives in a different world, and wonders how he should accommodate himself to it, or whether he should try. Perhaps he should take arms against the thing he sees. Perhaps he should labor to prove that freedom as he has known it will, if lost, be not well lost. Other civilizations have suffocated under their own dead weight, but this one of ours must not do so; and the secret of salvation lies in him. So he might say. And he would have to believe what he said. Also, he would have to understand it as he never understood it before. This freedom of which he speaks had better sound like a necessity. Sometimes it has sounded like a luxury which we could afford to indulge because we were rich and because the organization of our common life was comfortably loose; and because there was no great and present danger. Two world wars, and now the possibility of still another, have tightened our hearts more than many of us know and have shrunk the area in which freedom is supposed to play. But perhaps it is supposed to work. Freedom may be even more valuable than anybody has yet said. It may be our universal secret, bound to save us if we press out of it all its possible meaning. The time may have come to do just that—to persuade the people of our world that freedom is their own best good, and that if necessary they should pay for it as much as it will cost.

Its cost is measured by the danger it keeps alive: the danger from speculation and experiment. People may have to be persuaded that this is worth its weight in other gold than that of the familiar market; that the continuance of our culture depends upon its power to survive itself—if not in Greece, then in Rome, and if not in Rome, then in Paris, London, and New York—and that such power is found only in those societies which, while they love the truth, believe it to be always coming, and not here. But they must really love the truth; and the sign of this will be that they love all individuals who sincerely seek it. How sincere then will the artist have to be—how sincere, how humorous, and how profound? And how much more will he have to do in the present crisis than he has been doing in Europe and America over the past hundred years, when his subject matter has for the most part, and rather monotonously as it now appears, been the corruption and decay of modern life? The diagnosis was good, but the patient still waits upon his cure. The artist is not a physician, yet he had better be a thoughtful person. And in the current situation he had better be a person who knows what thought at the most can mean. The truth is not what anybody thinks. It is not even what the best of us think. It is still coming, and it will never be here. Meanwhile, and at any time, how much error can we afford? And how indifferent can we be to the deeper question of how we might live with the truth if we ever found it? These are tough questions, which the artist, like any responsible man, is answering even now as best he may. He is asking his world to gamble on him; and wondering, perhaps, if he is worth the risk.

He will be, it seems easy to say, as soon as his work is beautiful and good enough. Some of us could worry about this more than we do—not merely about our reward, but about what we are doing to deserve it. The artist may have to earn his freedom, with pictures and poems for which the world will gladly pay with some of its security. There could even be a poem for which a people would fight, as now they fight over insults and land. There could be a picture which society would dislocate itself to house and frame. There could be ideas that make ideologies look pale and hollow by comparison. The artist should be as ambitious as all that; should study, in addition to his own capacities, the capacities of his art itself, as if another practiced it and he stood by to see that all of its resources were remembered. We compete with our contemporaries more often than with the masters. What made them masters was that they remembered everything, and somehow put it in. The art of the novel suffers today from its leaving so much out. Most of its practitioners seem never to have read a great story, or any story at all. They have everything but what it takes to make a novel; and they complain of their reward. So, it may be, with other arts and artists. Ambition is a godlike thing, and men will worship it whenever it is supported by performance.

But ambition now might take on still another dimension—not a greater one, for nothing is greater than excellence, yet one that will serve excellence in the end. Society continues to change, and there are those who say it is already the monster we have feared. Whatever in truth it is, the artist ought to be one of the first to understand it, to sympathize with its predicament, and to start making it better at the core. He might even become a philosopher or a politician in order to do this well; but short of that, he can think more deeply and feelingly than he has done about the courage it now takes to be the sort of individual whose dignity matters more than wars and revolutions, more than welfare and the sovereignties of states. Such dignity is given to no one. It has to be created in the mind, by slow and painful stages, amid the total darkness of other men's refusal to make the attempt at all. But once it is created, it proves everything. And once it is created in an artist whose ambition is otherwise unbounded—and whose skill—it becomes the final excellence of which the rest of us had dreamed. It could even change again the changing world.

# The Kinds of Knowledge

WHEN a university, in the name of that knowledge to which it believes all men as men have right, reviews its own career of learning and of teaching, it is bound to ask itself what knowledge really is, and how much of it exists at present or can be imagined as existing in some day to come. Such a university, putting such a question to itself, will be expected to make a modest answer, for in no other place should the limits of the human mind be better known; but it is not required to deny that knowledge exists at all, or to suggest, if knowledge be supposed to exist in several kinds, that these are like the kinds of snakes in Ireland: varieties of nothing in the end.

The university has faith in knowledge. Or to put the case more accurately, it has faith in the possibility of knowledge. The possibility is what matters, plus a method, or a set of methods, whereby the actuality may in ever higher and higher degree be encouraged to exist. Those to whom the problem is not real assume the actuality already to exist: somewhere, somehow, someone knows everything. But to others it is a familiar fact that the true scholar is more interested in what he may know tomorrow than in what he knows today, and is more likely to want to talk about it. The modesty of the true scholar is neither a gesture nor a joke. To him it is quite literally the case that a science of anything presupposes a vast ignorance concerning it: an ignorance, indeed, so vast that even its very nature may never be understood. He as a scientist, in other words, may never become clear as to what it is of which he is ignorant, or ought to consider himself ignorant; he may never learn just what it is that he should seek to know. Meanwhile, however, he has his method; he does know how to proceed within the field of ignorance he has managed to define. And that one field is vast enough; nor will all of it, perhaps, be ever conquered. So he is always busy, with scarcely the time to pause and tell us, should we ask, how much he knows; and more particularly, how much of what he knows.

To the extent that he is a true scholar he will contemplate this question of the what, and seriously ask it of himself. Is he studying the right thing?—which means, for true scholars, the most difficult, the most hidden, the most abstract, the most inaccessible thing. Has he been content thus far with fields of ignorance that others have defined? Has he discovered any for himself? And if he has, is it the farthest field, beyond whose fences, conceivably, the simple truth sits looking at itself? Often this farthest field seems nearest to the uninitiated mind, which asks elementary questions about it: What is it, after all? Why are you studying it? What would it mean to know what you say you want to know? What difference will it make? Or, in a more friendly voice, even an eager one: What is electricity? What is life? What is poetry? Can history be true, and if so, what history is most true? Is there such a thing as human nature, and does it grow? What is government? What is law? What is money? What are the stars, and why is there so much space between them? Where is God? And if men knew everything, would they be God?

The truest scholar will be the most tolerant of such questions, for they are like the ones he asks himself when he is simple and serious; and if he is never simple and serious, he is a pedant or a quack, and the long face he wears as he discourses on his method is a sign that he does not know why he has it, or what he will do with the results of it when he gets them. Universities have their share of persons who practice learning without a divine license; who do not know what is important unless someone else tells them; who work in fields of ignorance from which for them there is no escape; who labor in the dark to raise ever higher and higher the heap of little fragments which in their boastful moments they call the sum of human knowledge.

But what is the sum of human knowledge? Or what would it be if it ever were complete? And is it necessarily a future thing, something to be hoped for only, something impossible now? Can one be certain that it does not already exist? If it needs to be the equivalent of God's knowledge, certainly it does not exist; for men are neither more nor less divine than they originally were. But doubtless there is no such need. Men may know merely what men can know. And according to one view they have always known it. Jonathan Swift thought men knew it in his time, two centuries and more ago. But most of them, he concluded, were not aware that they knew it, and so had got lost in mazes of speculation and experiment for which there was no earthly use—nor divine use either, since God does not find it necessary to be a scientist, a philosopher, or a theologian. These are human terms, less admirable for Swift than the monosyllable *man*. Most men in any time, he said, know all that can be known about how to live and how not to live; it is only sickness, or corruption, or perversity that cuts them off from life itself, which everywhere is simple and makes no mystery of its rules. Liars are liars in any world; and so are hypocrites and thieves, and lazy people; and so are the lovely people—the kind, the just, the generous, the temperate, the courageous, the wise, the strong.

There is validity in such a view. Men's thoughts about themselves are different from one decade to the next, but their virtues and their vices do not seem to change. The very man who tries to prove that there is no longer any distinction between good and bad—that these are words, not things—will in his next breath denounce a neighbor of whose conduct he disapproves. The very man who swears that it is old-fashioned to speak of truth may find himself, before the day is over, calling some other man a falsifier. Most of us, it may be, know more than we admit; we know, as Swift said, how to live; at least we keep on living, as our great-grandfathers did. And this regardless of whether or not we have access to the kinds of knowledge with which universities are concerned.

And properly concerned. For the possibilities of knowledge which haunt and inspire scholars are themselves among the things that prove man human. Not animal, certainly, since animals know perfectly how they should live in order to survive and to repeat themselves. Not godlike, just as certainly; for the possibilities can never be more than possibilities. And if Swift with all his genius could despise them, so we too may remember how they limit us; we too may learn from him and them how not to be too proud.

Yet they are half the truth about mankind. To be a scholar is not to be an unnatural thing. The nature of man is to want more knowledge than he will ever possess, and to work for it as if it still might be possessed. And if in his universities he gives that knowledge a variety of names, if he recognizes it in more than a single form, he does not in so doing deny that the many may be one, or might be if a proper view of them could be obtained. Perhaps in our day he tries less hard than once he did to master the perspectives that would be involved in such a complete and distant view of himself in the act of contemplation. His nature does not, it would seem, permit him to do this; yet he has made the attempt, and he will make it again. At the moment, however, he looks as if he lacked the ambition, not to say the curiosity. We do not hear him asking what it is, if it is anything, that the poet and the mathematician know together, or the historian and the chemist, or the musician and the doctor, or the moral philosopher and the atomic physicist. The sum of human knowledge, were it attainable and statable, might be a single sentence, a single word; or it might be only so clear a view of everything that sound was superogatory, and speech an impertinence. Granted that the sum is inaccessible, man still may speculate as to its parts, and as to the niceties of their relation. Contemporary man, at least in universities, refuses to do so. He lets the study of literature be altogether different from the study of bacteria and the stars. If some resemblance actually is there, he does not know of it because he has never inquired. He assumes a perfect absence of relation; and so if he is a student of poetry he is content with total ignorance of energy, proportion, and equation, though poetry is built of just those things; and if he is a natural scientist he does not stop to wonder whether it is more than a coincidence that art must be natural too, or must seem so if it would exert its utmost force; nor does he ask that force to confess any resemblance it may bear to gravity and whirlwinds, to natural selection and a mushroom cloud.

But even if he did this, and even if the poet were better educated than he is, the answer would never come, we may be sure, in the form of one apocalyptic word. The knowledge of such a word which the theologian has is another kind of knowledge, unsupported by what is ordinarily called evidence, either in universities or in the outer world; but especially in universities, whose scholars are experts in evidence, and grow wary at once if told that something is true although it never can be proved. Yet revelation belongs in their lives too, as it belongs in the career of every healthy intellect, no matter what the training it has had, and whether this be great or small. Any man knows things he has not been told; the good teacher gives forth more than he was taught; sometimes the truth comes easily, as if it said itself. And this can be the case whatever the theory of knowledge one professes—Swift's or that of the most methodical scholar. The knowledge that advances, like the knowledge that stands still, is studded with discoveries which cannot be traced to any source. It is vanity to deny this, and folly to underrate it. Nor is it the same thing as that apocalyptic word which is never to be spoken. It used to be understood that the knowledge of angels came with less difficulty than that of men. It came instantaneously, whereas for men it was the labor of a lifetime to learn the little that they knew. Men still are less than the angels, and what they know is of a lower order; yet any man, on any occasion, may be more wise than he is able to explain. The name for this is brilliance: a sudden light that no one has turned on. And it can come on anywhere: in the laboratory, the recitation hall, the midnight study; in the field, the street, the noisy or the quiet room; in sleep, or at the hour of waking, or halfway through an otherwise eventless day. It too is knowledge, though it never has been earned.

Most human knowledge, nevertheless, comes hard. Either it distills itself painfully out of common experience, or it subjects the scholar, its uncommon devotee, to excruciating efforts of observation and close thought. Seldom if ever does inspiration come without such fiery trials before it, and even then it may not come; but if it does, it has to that extent been earned, and is deserved. The university does not count upon its coming, any more than it lays out work in the expectation that only geniuses will do it. Miracles and geniuses are rare in any world, and it is the part of wisdom not to await them. The academic life is bound to be laborious, however many or few the kinds of knowledge it is lived for. It is not as dull as some men think it, but it is duller than a circus or a battlefield; and so it ought to be, since neither in game nor in earnest is it lived in defiance of death. The definition of all life is rather its province: all life, whose most exciting secrets it has no mandate to unearth. To define a thing is not in so far to possess it. The clearest definition of life would be the completest statement of what it is not. Life itself, the individual thing, prefers to be known for what it is; and those who have known it the most directly may be the least articulate about its essence. Its essence, tragic or comic, the university is under no obligation to reveal.

But to say this is not to justify the vulgar charge that academic life is unreal life. It is as real as definition is; as useful, and as clear. In an ideal world the privilege of experience and the duty of understanding would doubtless not exclude each other. Nor in the world we have do they do so altogether; if they could, neither one of them would then make sense. The pure thing and the pure word are not for men as men are made. So the university continues to be looked to for more than dry information and dead fact; for more, even, than the cold light of clearest comprehension. It is looked to for wisdom, a warmer and a wilder thing than any of those. And often enough wisdom is there; nor does it seem too different from the wisdom of the great world, begotten by virtue upon the body of experience. The scholar is not forbidden to have experience; he is a man too, and loves and hates and undergoes ambition. At his worst, if the extreme case be considered, he is unable to make his humanity appear; it was weak to begin with, as could have been true of any man, or else he has darkened it and dampened it with cellar growths which have shut him away at last from the sun and from all things that the sun makes clear to normal men. But in the best cases, and happily these are numerous, he has been rendered more sensible, not less so, by the education he has given himself and others. He has become, that is to say, more practical. He has become a man of whom other men will not hesitate to ask advice. In the best world we have any right to expect, the scholar and the citizen will freely converse, will freely compare experience, and will freely tell each other how to live. Not that the distinction between them will have disappeared. It is a rich distinction, not to be minimized in any world that wants to keep on being simple and serious. But talking will take place; and all the kinds of knowledge may then lie down with one another.

# The Names of Greece

THE GLORY that was Greece survives, we said, in its place names. The Orient Express had toiled all night, all day, through Yugoslavia where no shape or label was familiar, and where the inhabitants, stolid at best, looked even more so beneath the burden, borne to be sure with impressive patience, of an anonymity as blank as that of the muddy slopes over which they drove their spotted cows, substitutes for oxen.

Then suddenly, on Thursday evening, the train stopped at a little station in front of which men sat at tables, smiling and talking while waiters brought them thimblefuls of coffee and towering glasses of clear water. There were no guards with pistols, and somewhere music played. At last we were in Greece; and there was brightness in the air. These men knew where they lived, and who they were; and obviously they liked it, as by instinct we did too.

If we had leaned out to ask them whether we would see Olympus as we passed they would certainly have known that we would not; nor Pieria, nor the Vale of Tempe, nor the nearby peninsula where golden apples still are grown and still are called Hesperides. No, we were not to see daylight until the plains of Thessaly were behind us. But after breakfast a high, handsome mountain rose on the right, and as I stood in the corridor admiring it the porter came softly to my side and said: "Parnassus," and when I showed my pleasure showed his pride. Nor had many minutes gone before the train slowed down for a village and I made out of the letters on the station sign no less luminous a word than Helicon.

Parnassus, Helicon; and in another hour or so there would be Thebes. The names said themselves over and over in my ears: a marvelous music, suitable somehow to a swiftly unfolding landscape brilliant everywhere with its own natural sculpture, and to a race of women on the hills—slender women, conscious of their grace—who rode small donkeys debonairly, their feet swinging, their red blouses and white kerchiefs blowing as they descended to pick cotton in miniature fields where their dark husbands already stood, waving at the train as if it were something that did not pass them every morning.

So here we were. And every day after this, for the more than two weeks that we had in Greece, I repeated my discovery: its glory is its names—of places and of persons, on earth or in the sky. For the incomparable people who once lived here had a myth-making power, which is to say a poetic power, such as no other people has ever had, unless indeed the ancient Hebrews, with their Hebron and their Jordan, their Moses and their David, had as much. But surely even then it cannot be true, I thought, that any other country, big or little, has given the world so many magic words to say, so many actions to remember. The words and the actions, the names and the legends, went together in the great Greece that has disappeared; they danced as one in a deeply colored world shot through with mind that penetrated everywhere, delighting in all forms of thought and feeling.

And yet great Greece has never disappeared, since if nothing else the names it lived with have survived. Hephaestus, for example, my favorite among its gods, who limped at his forge because Zeus in a fit of anger once threw him down from Olympus and he broke his left leg falling "on Lemnos, the Aegean isle," has not been forgotten. I have two evidences for this. One afternoon in Athens we were walking through a narrow street which all at once grew narrower still, and we became aware of blacksmith shops on both sides of us: dark caves of stone in which hammers rang and white fire blazed in forges kept alive by huge hand-operated bellows. Iron and bronze were being worked by men in leather aprons, and I thought of sundry gold objects that the lame smith-god had fashioned for the heroes and the gods: Achilles' shield, for instance, and the cups from which the Olympians drank their nectar. The companions of the divine artificer laughed at his lameness, Homer tells us; probably they despised him because he worked with his hands, or because he worked at all. And to be sure he was swarthy as well as lame, and built closer to the ground than beautiful cruel Apollo or the implacable Aphrodite with her snow-white arms and shoulders (his own wife, in fact, and she was untrue to him with Ares, god of war; but that is another story). Well, I glanced up to see where we were so that we could come this way again, and the sign said, of all things, "Hephaestus Street." I learned the next day that we had been at the bottom of the north slope of the hill on which the temple of Hephaestus stands overlooking the Agora —and so has stood for two millenniums; an archaeologist assured me that the name was no coincidence.

Then in Arcadia, when our driver was crossing a dizzy range of mountains and the radiator sprang a serious leak, we found it necessary to stop in a village where the blacksmith was reputed to be skillful with solder. He was indeed, and we worked the bellows for him while the entire population gathered to watch both him and us—us, certainly, for we were strangers and their curiosity about us was at least as strong as the sense of hospitality which moved them to bring us chairs and a little table to eat our lunch on in the street. The smith, who would not proceed with the mending until he had shared his own lunch with the driver, at last got down to work; and he did it so well that in admiration I said to him the one word I considered relevant: "Hephaestus." His teeth gleamed as he tapped his chest, nodded energetically, and corrected my accent: "Eéphestos!" This was as good as being in Arcadia, not many miles north of Sparta where Helen lived (except for ten years) with Menelaus; or northwest of sandy Pylos, where young Telemachus came in his chariot to ask what Nestor knew of his father Odysseus; or southwest of Mycenae where Agamemnon once was king of men. As good, I say, as being in Arcadia, though I saw nothing of its most famous inhabitant, goat-foot Pan.

Pan is not there, and of course in Sparta there is no visible suggestion of Leda whose experience with an immortal swan produced Helen, the most beautiful of women. Even no trace is there of the dour folk whose only god was discipline, and who won their fatal war with Athens. Thucydides' prediction about them has long since come true; possessing no ideas and no art, they have utterly disappeared; so the Athenians with their intellectual goddess and their innumerable poets and philosophers have at last the perfect revenge: their city is the metropolis and capital of living Greece.

Athens itself is certainly alive. In fact we sometimes thought it too much so; it seemed feverish and intense, with dust blowing in the streets and a thousand drivers doing their demon best to run us down. Doubtless it was thus when Socrates stood calmly in the Stoa of Zeus and infuriated the sophists who were no cleverer than he and infinitely less serious. It is always dangerous to be serious in the pursuit of truth, and most men then as well as now avoided the kind of death their master died. Most men in Athens now are talkers. And what talkers! Constitution Square boils and buzzes with them every evening before the late dinner the Athenians like. So far as I know it is the biggest area on earth devoted entirely to coffee and conversation, and tonguewise it is the busiest. Politics or love, money or religion—no matter what the theme, the eloquence (with gestures) is enormous. Perhaps they never truly argue, meeting point with point; I have read somewhere that each of them desires only to erect a taller column of words than his neighbor can, and as such more admirable; and if like children's blocks they all topple at last, no one especially cares, for bright new piles, false at the worst, specious at the best, can easily rise again.

Athens is not so much a city as a vast, overgrown town. I was told in the Chamber of Commerce that every Greek now wants to live there, and that too many have come. Certainly the view from Lycabettus or the Acropolis is of white buildings flowing as far as one can see like foam among the hills. But nowhere is there the appearance of power, of sumptuous majesty, such as even the meaner streets of Rome somehow support. The greatness of this Greece was long ago; it departed in the Dark and Middle Ages either east to Constantinople or west to the city of the seven hills. Athens degenerated into a village at the feet of the Acropolis; and if it is large again, it is still a village. Only monuments—the Parthenon on high, the temples of Olympian Zeus and Hephaestus lower down—remain to prove how measureless the might of Athens was in its own bit of time. Its wealth then, and its profundity of wit—its prowess in myth, in idea, in the bestowing of imperishable names—the mystery of these is deeper than any ever guarded at Eleusis, today a suburb surrounded by soap factories. To go there by the Sacred Way is to end up among ruins—scattered fragments of columns such as at last become routine for tourists in Greece. The rubble is convincing, but it is also heartbreaking. So much glory, so utterly gone.

The mountains and the plains are as stunning as ever; but at Delphi, say, where are the votaries for whom the Castalian Spring is an effective rite before they proceed to the oracle? Where is the Pythoness, and where is the gold that once lay heaped in the treasuries? Where is the slave who struggles to arrive and touch this holy ground so that henceforth he may be forever free? Where is the sense that Delphi keeps the secret, unknown to even the wisest city-states, of permanent peace? Eagles still soar between the summit of Parnassus and the Corinthian Gulf, but they look down upon a desert of human history. So at Olympia, across the Gulf: cyclopean drums of fallen columns lie everywhere among huge trees, but where are the brilliant athletes who for a thousand years competed here for laurel and the praise of poets? The river whose floods have carved away the stadium—"Return, Alpheus, the dread voice is past that shrunk thy streams"—meanders through gravel with no memory of the shouts and prayers it used to overhear. At Mycenae the tombs of Agamemnon and Clytemnestra—or, some say, of Perseus and Andromeda—are beehive holes in little hills from whose tops there is nothing to see but the burnt tops of bigger mountains, or in one direction the Argive plain where it is quite impossible even to imagine the chariot of Agamemnon bearing him to his bloody death at the hands of Clytemnestra and her paramour. How can Cassandra, princess and prophetess, be ever so faintly made out as she stands behind her new master, shrieking because she knows he will be murdered? And where is Pelops' line for whom the peninsula is named—Atreus and Thyestes, barbarous brothers whose sons still hate each other?

Orestes went wandering from here pursued by the Furies because he had killed his mother; but we did not see him at Delphi, clinging to the base of Apollo's statue, nor in Athens was it thinkable that the Areopagus ever witnessed the trial by which at last he was acquitted. So up in Thebes, the town we passed through on the train, there was no feeblest vestige of the place where Oedipus discovered his guilt and Jocasta hanged herself; of the gates—there are no gates—beyond which Polyneices and Eteocles slew each other, and Antigone was forbidden to bury her brother's body; or of the still older city built by Cadmus, where Zeus visited Semele in a bolt of lightning and Pentheus was torn to pieces by Agave, who thought him a beast and herself inspired. Outside the city Cithaeron still heaves its slopes on one of which the infant Oedipus was exposed to die, and on toward Delphi there is the place in the mountains where three roads meet and Laius, angrily contesting the right of way, was killed by his accursed son. But whether here or off in rocky Ithaca which once awaited its returning lord, or north by Olympus, or east among the shining Cyclades that still appear to revolve about Delos, their sacred center, the glory lives only in the sound of syllables a modern Greek, it sometimes seems, outrageously mispronounces.

Not that the modern Greek is unworthy of full praise. For one thing he has kept the names, and is proud to note that we come five thousand miles to hear them spoken. But better yet, he is hospitable and kind, and his ever-present smile is as sweet as it could be if he were richer than he is. He is certainly poor; yet among the valleys of Arcadia—much deeper and grander than I had thought—he looks at you as you pass and returns your greeting in triple measure. So does his wife—often she is beautiful, with serious dark eyes—as she jogs home at sunset on her donkey from the fields. And so do his children, who may bring you flowers to smell (perhaps also to buy), but who in any case will stare at you with a solemn consuming curiosity, as if it still were true that you could be a god come through their village in disguise. All of them are courteous, and concerned about your comfort. I shall not forget the little boy in Heraklion, chief port of Crete, who as I stood wearily in front of our hotel, waiting for the bags to come down, tapped me on the shoulder and showed me a rickety chair he had dragged from some doorway for my use. Neither shall I forget the mistake I made in offering him a drachma. He shook his head and grinned. It had been a ritual, not a transaction.

We had gone to Crete, of course, to see the palace at Cnossus. Yet, splendid as it is (or was), I shall keep uppermost in mind not only this boy but an ancient couple farther inland at whose tavern our driver stopped so that we could drink country wine. I say tavern; it was only their small house, by a bridge that crossed a dry stream under a gigantic plane tree which our host assured us was five hundred years old. He had lost one eye, and so had his yellow cat; and his wife hobbled on feet that evidently hurt her as she set out, in addition to the wine, cups of bitter coffee and the inevitable tumblers of water, then after that a plate of veal deliciously soaked in the juices of onions and red peppers. The two of them stood and watched us enjoy what may in fact have been their lunch. And they did accept some drachmas in return. But we could not have paid for their beaming faces as they bowed us out to the car, whose driver stopped twice on the way back to Heraklion, once to pick a bunch of grapes from a vineyard he heard us praising, and again to tell us (in terrible English) how he had been a captain of Partisans resisting the Germans between 1941 and 1945, and how on this very bridge–he got out to show us, pointing down–an enemy general had been thrown into the river. He was happy to conduct us to the Labyrinth of Minos, but he insisted too that we see how the Greeks of his time had made history. So they had, and so they will forever, those charming people with the white teeth who know so well the names of their predecessors.

# Robert Herrick Revisited

IT BEGAN in Cambridge. The master of one of the oldest colleges, in the midst of a conversation about the changes that have come over England, the universities, and all of the modern world, said suddenly: "Lyric poetry, you know, is now a mere survival." I said I didn't know it, and he went on to still more dismal subjects. But the death of lyric poetry, evidently a grimmer possibility for me than for the master, since he seemed to forget what he had said and could not be drawn back into argument, was something I thought about for days. Then I remembered Herrick, a lyric poet if anyone ever was, and I wished I had cited his case. For the poems of Herrick died, then lived again. His one book, *Hesperides and Noble Numbers*, attracted little attention in 1648 when it was published; was ignored for the rest of its century and for all of the one that followed; and was not reprinted until 1810. Since then, of course, it has enjoyed innumerable editions, and so many people know by heart so many of its delicious lines that its bibliography is scarcely to be believed. Yet there it is, sufficient proof that a poet can be reborn.

Doubtless in 1648 this poet whom we think we cannot do without looked like a mere survival of quiet, sweet days before the flood of revolution and civil war. Herrick was classical, was a literary son of Ben Jonson, and through him of Horace, Martial, Ovid, and Catullus; also, he was a Royalist, faithful to King Charles who in another year would lose his head; and worse yet he was a vicar in the Church of England, or he had been until the loss of his living a year ago. Then he had come up from a remote village in Devon to publish in London the work of his life thus far; he was fifty-six, and unemployed. And London, busy with becoming modern, had little interest in a book that should have been published twenty years before. It had no time for lyric poems, no ear for songs that might have been proper in some springtime of the world. Now it was hot summer—even wild autumn, even dead winter—and the gathering of rosebuds was a quaint game for children, not to be revived.

London was wrong then, judging by the remarkable way in which it reversed itself a hundred and sixty-two years later; and so, I told myself, it might be wrong now—or my friend in Cambridge might, not to speak of all those in America who periodically announce the deaths of deathless things. We shall know the answer in time, I said—perhaps in a good deal of time—but meanwhile, what about a trip to Dean Prior, in Devon, where Herrick had his living, and where he inhabited, by the testimony of at least a dozen poems, so small a house that the very weather of three hundred years might have worn it away? The church, however, would be there, and the meadows where Herrick walked, and the modest streams beside whose banks he witnessed the brief careers of flowers:

> Fair daffodils, we weep to see
> You haste away so soon.

So on a windy, showery day in late September we drove down. I admitted all the way that such a visit made no special sense. It is never necessary to be in body where a poet was in mind; furthermore, since he was a highly trained artist, Herrick had continued to see in Devon what Horace and Ben Jonson had taught him to see in London and Rome, and what this was we can see for ourselves in his perfect poems, which could have been written anywhere on earth once their creator was free of the earth as only art could free him. Further still, he hated Devon. Or he said he did. For him it was a place of exile, days or weeks away from the streets and courts where he had once been used to drink the heady wines and to catch in flight the winged words of the capital in which he was born. A goldsmith's son and then a student of law, and after that a poet whose pieces got into the best contemporary collections, he had been forced at forty to accept this distant benefice if he was to live at all.

But like Swift, who said he had been sent to Dublin "to die like a rat in a hole," Herrick affected to despise Dean Prior. Perhaps he really did; doubtless no brilliant people were there, and his epigrams describe some dreadfully unattractive habits in certain yeomen of the vicinity. It was a dull place, he said, and loathsome. He was an old bachelor, again like Swift; and like Swift too he was possessed of a wit that would never let him *seem* to be pleased with where he was. I have always supposed that he did like Devon after all, with an affection such as strong men can still have for life when it has lost its strangeness. Nevertheless he might have said: "For God's sake, don't come down. My little house is less than nothing, and the one maid I have is but a country maid—a good girl, but no manners." This would be Prudence Baldwin, whom several of his poems celebrate and whom he must have warmly liked. He wouldn't have expected us, I thought, to take him at his word and stay away.

Also, he had his mistresses. Or he said he did. Julia, Anthea, Perilla, Perenna, Lucia, and the rest—their Latin names can make us wonder if they were more than literary relatives of Horace's Lydia and the Lesbia of Catullus. Not that they were therefore the less real; the liquefaction of Julia's clothes, the sweet disorder in another's dress, the stately hair of still another when she was costumed to his liking are realities for us at any rate, and for all we care the ladies lived.

This man must have had many secrets, not the least of which was that he wrote verses. Who else in Dean Prior knew? The vicar was a huge, ugly man with a hooked nose and a mop of curly black hair that fitted his head like a wrestler's cap. Who then, seeing him every day, would have guessed the delicacy of his musician's touch, the cunning of his mind when he set out to carve the lyrics that will keep their shape forever? His passion was poetry, there can be no doubt of that; and if he loved a dozen girls he loved as many poets quite as fondly, and wore them in his inmost heart where he worshiped them either in the direct way of praise or in the devious way of imitation.

> Ah, Ben!
> Say how or when
> Shall we, thy guests,
> Meet at those lyric feasts
> Made at the Sun,
> The Dog, the Triple Tun?
> Where we such clusters had,
> As made us nobly wild, not mad;
> And yet each verse of thine
> Out-did the meat, out-did the frolic wine.

He never forgot his English master who would permit no falseness in the note, no dullness in the file, and who himself, despite his brutal size and his bully manners, had written "Drink to Me only with Thine Eyes."

The richest of Herrick's secrets may have been the art he continued in the desert of Devon to practice as if he were still a free citizen of poetry's entire world, resolving never to falter or to let his craft decay, and finding subjects where no subjects ought to be. For here they were after all, in the purlieus of his exile: brooks, fields, and country wassails, and a rosebush by a rock, along with the high color in Perilla's cheeks, and the importunity of desire, and (alas!) the signs in him of old age when performance was to be outlived; and the meannesses, some of them quite filthy, that he found in his parishioners, whom he railed at in a hundred epigrams —copied, to be sure, out of Martial—now often dropped from chaste editions of his work, to our loss and to his. For nothing human was alien to this man, and he put everything into the book he took to London when he thought his exile was over. It was not over; he was to return when another Charles was king and was to spend twelve more years in Devon before he died at eighty-three—for all we know without again touching pen to paper, though it may be that the poems of his old age were buried with him.

Even before he left, however, he had written *Noble Numbers* as well as the *Hesperides,* and the printer bound both books together. The second, the religious one, is no less happy than the first, and no less wonderful. Perhaps his very deepest secret was the way he could pass in the same hour from pagan fantasy to sober meditation, just as he could entertain at the same instant, or at least with the same mind, the hue of violets and the foulness of some yokel's breath. Like Swift again (Swift's mother, it may be time to say, was born a Herrick) he shrank from dirt—perhaps too far and too fastidiously. Yet no one who has read every word of him will wish him different. We are glad he left no manuscripts behind him when he took the long ride to London. We can only wonder how many of his neighbors knew about the book when he came back, a man of seventy-one, to resume his ways and walks. "There he goes, the poet parson. What is he thinking now?" We can hope that the secret was kept until the end.

Dean Prior, when we found it on that dripping day, had no appearance of a literary shrine. England is rich in these, and can afford to leave the tally incomplete. For me at least it was just as well; I preferred to find my way alone—past the thatched village, then another mile along the Plymouth highway until Herrick's church, grey and unprepossessing, showed up among some wet trees on the left. We entered its yard by a rusty gate and walked between weeds to a door that few strangers ever enter. Inside, the spectacle was neat but poor: no splendor anywhere, and little color except in a modern window above the altar which was to be sure a Herrick window, with his gross likeness in one of its lower corners and some fragments of his verse curling in ribbons across the whole design. I was more touched by a card hung on a pillar, saying in effect that we who had come here because Robert Herrick once was vicar were entreated to pray for the present incumbent and his living people. But I was most touched, as I turned to see what the rear wall was like, by these four lines on a piece of wood that I think the present incumbent must have put there, for it bore no marks of age:

In this little urn is laid
Prudence Baldwin, once my maid,
From whose happy spark here let
Spring the purple violet.

Not that Herrick himself had ever seen this best of all his epitaphs in place. Prue did not die until 1678, four years after her master, perhaps with her help, was lowered into his grave outside the church. We shall never know why he wrote the lines: whether in pure affection, or to see if he could, or because the subject of them had requested that he do so—even, on some winter evening, dared him to. In any case their art is such that they contain as in a tiny glass the essence of both the vicar and the maid.

A young woman was playing the organ, and when she stopped she informed us that the vicar was away in Exeter for the day. She only practiced there, she said. And where was Herrick's house? Why, just across from the gate we had come in by. She was going there now, and she would take us. I said I had thought it too big, and she laughed. "Oh, other vicars have enlarged it. But Herrick's part *was* little—you can see—I live in that."

It was quite as he had described it, at least as regards dimension. A few boxes of rooms, and out of one door a miniature garden, no longer well kept. Here Herrick had hidden for thirty years, here prayed, here eaten, and here relished versing, as George Herbert puts it. Here he had been tended by Prue; here he was called on by persons of the parish who perhaps had found him strange at first; here, sitting alone, or it may be with some companion who was in on his secret, upon occasion he raised his glass in a toast to those long dead who were his bosom friends, the lyric poets who for him were not dead after all, nor mere survivals either. One of his finest poems is such a toast, bearing the infectious title "To Live Merrily and to Trust to Good Verses."

Then this immensive cup
  Of aromatic wine,
Catullus, I quaff up
  To that terse Muse of thine.

To trust to good verses. That would have been his answer to anyone who asked him how important lyric poetry was in those terrible times. Perhaps all times are terrible, but some are clearly so, and they are the very ones when we should drink to the imperishable line, the music that nothing muffles. If Herrick were here now and we asked him how much chance our poetry had to be remembered in the future, it would be his right to ask in turn: "What poetry have you got?" And he would examine what we showed him with a view to the perfection of its sound and sense. Perfection, that is to say, if any. For perfection is a rare commodity, as he knew better than most men. It appears but here and there; almost never in whole poems, though that is possible too; more probably in the sudden witty, sweet phrase which labor and good luck have generated between them. It was such phrases, such turns of thought, that made him tremble when he found them, either on the paper before him or in the volumes of his masters. Nothing mattered to him more. And if when he published his own book he admitted many pieces he knew to be imperfect, I fancy it was for a human reason that I like in him as much as I like the best of his poetry: he was fond of the places or the persons they were about. He trusted us, I mean, to find the pure gold on the other pages, as indeed we have. The best-known poems of Herrick are the best. They tend to be the best, too, of their kind in any language.

They are so good, I sometimes think, that criticism is at a loss before them. Criticism now at any rate. For we have fallen out of love with lightness, we are worried by a poet's wit. As critics we prefer the solemn or confused author whose mind it is easy to enter because in despair he has left it open. The better artist conceals his mind, as he wants us to conceal ours, in the service of a third thing, the subject, which stands between us, and which he would convert into a product —a poem in the present case—more interesting than either him or us. In proportion as any poet approaches this goal he is perfect, he is classic. Or to put it bluntly, he is successful.

But criticism shies these days from the spectacle of success. Shakespeare and Mozart, who really finished their thought and left it to be ours if we can take it, are seldom considered in terms of their success. Their blazing triumphs are hardly ever looked at face to face and talked about with the courage that living with masterpieces requires. So Horace, whose select and rare felicity is one of the few things worth a critic's attention, is assumed instead of discussed. And Herrick, his faultless pupil, is passed over for the very reason that in so many poems he was perfect–which is the precise place for criticism to begin. Not that it is easy to go on from there. It is almost as difficult to talk well about a good poem as it is to write one. Yet we can try.

# Index

¶ This book is set in Janson, a type face designed by Anton Janson, a Dutch letter founder. Little is known about Janson and his work. He settled in Leipzig around 1670, and issued his first specimen sheet about 1675. This face gives a feeling of compactness and sturdiness; it is legible even in its smaller sizes. ¶ This book was designed by Myrtle Powell, and composed, printed and bound by American Book–Stratford Press.